Hope Is Here!

Hope Is Here! is designed for congregational, communal, or small-group use. To assist groups using the book, we've developed a free, downloadable congregational guide, which includes reflections on the lessons in the book; Scripture references from the Old and New Testaments and prayers, which can be used in study, devotion, or preaching opportunities; practical applications of the spiritual practices found in the book; and space to work together to create congregational commitments. Visit **www.wjkbooks.com/HopeIsHere** to download these resources.

"*Hope Is Here!* is an invitation with a trumpet sound. Luther Smith offers his testimony born from years of adventure, revelation, and contemplation on the revolutionary power of hope. Herein is a glimpse of the expansive depth and inclusivity of the prophetic force of hope. Hope is shown as the agency of the Divine that is always present, purposeful, transformative, persistent, inclusive, boundary breaking, prophetic, and invitational. Hope is not a commodity to be possessed; it possesses us. In this novel book, Smith invites us on a journey of experiencing and exploring the source, depth, and possibilities of hope's transformative power in the lives of individuals as well as the agenda of justice and the vision of the future of community. Furthermore, given the human tendency to resist hope, Smith invites everyone to embrace a contemplative journey propelled by the ongoing practice of the spiritual disciplines that facilitate receptivity to living out the gift of God's hope and expanding the human capacity to be agents for justice and builders of the beloved community. *Hope Is Here!* is a wake-up call to all persons, regardless of their ideological or theological bent. Here is a book for the ages, indeed the future of humanity."

—**Thomas Louis Brown Sr.**, Presiding Bishop, Sixth Episcopal District, Christian Methodist Episcopal Church

"As we continue to work toward the elusive goal of Martin Luther King Jr.'s beloved community, what is the role of hope? Does hope energize us in the struggle for justice, or is it a form of wishful thinking that allows us to evade the fierce urgency of now? In this pivotal book, Luther E. Smith Jr.—drawing on his long, rich, and distinguished career as a teacher, scholar, preacher, and activist—reframes this question with the claim that hope is not a feeling but a force, a transformative 'force of God that enlivens us to life.' His evidence for that claim is compelling: story after story of people he calls 'witnesses' whose lives are animated by the power of hope. For Smith, these people are not mere case studies. They are hope incarnate, and they embody the possibility that we, too, may grow into the word of hope become flesh. As one who has sometimes felt distant from hope, this book has helped me understand that hope is never distant from me. May it do the same for you."

—**Parker J. Palmer**, author of *Let Your Life Speak*, *A Hidden Wholeness*, and *Healing the Heart of Democracy*

"Luther Smith's new book is a luminous portrait of the spiritual underpinnings of social justice, nonviolence, and the theological virtue of hope. In lucid prose, he knits his years of wisdom to create concrete examples of love in action. Hope is not only an optimistic anticipation of a good outcome but also a profound practice for the creation of beloved community. Read this book and be inspired!"

—**Wendy Farley**, Rice Family Chair of Spirituality,
San Francisco Theological Seminary,
Graduate School of Theology, Redlands University

"Luther has given us a timely and much-needed gift with this book. He offers a robust and trustworthy understanding of hope that is worthy of the call to follow Jesus in bringing good news to the poor, sight to the blind, and liberty to the oppressed. All of which are very much needed today. Moreover, the book is full of practical insights and wisdom, describing practices that can help us to live in and from such hope. In short, *Hope Is Here!* gives me courage, and I am grateful. If you're seeking support in sustaining courage and aliveness to life, read this book."

—**Johnny Sears**, Director, The Academy for
Spiritual Formation, The Upper Room

"Luther Smith is the voice of wisdom we all need. This wonderful book revitalizes our understanding of hope and its transformative power, integrating peace and justice, self and community, social action and contemplation. *Hope Is Here!* is a life-giving and soul-nourishing read for everyone committed to the beloved community."

—**Ellen Ott Marshall**, Professor of Christian Ethics
and Conflict Transformation, Candler School
of Theology, Emory University

Hope Is Here!

Spiritual Practices for Pursuing
Justice and Beloved Community

LUTHER E. SMITH JR.

WESTMINSTER
JOHN KNOX PRESS
LOUISVILLE • KENTUCKY

First edition
Published by Westminster John Knox Press
Louisville, Kentucky

23 24 25 26 27 28 29 30 31 32—10 9 8 7 6 5 4 3 2 1

Scripture quotations are from the New Revised Standard Version, Updated Edition. Copyright © 2021 National Council of Churches of Christ in the United States of America. Used by permission. All rights reserved worldwide. Scripture quotations marked RSV are from the Revised Standard Version of the Bible, copyright © 1946, 1952, 1971, and 1973 by the Division of Christian Education of the National Council of the Churches of Christ in the U.S.A., and are used by permission.

Excerpt from "Revealing Pain Undoes a Social Fiction," *Emory Report*, April 21, 2008, is reprinted by permission of Terry Eiesland. Excerpt from "I Will Sing a New Song," in *The Mood of Christmas* by Howard Thurman, is reprinted by permission of Friends United Press. Copyright 1973 by Howard Thurman. All rights reserved. Quote from Eknath Easwaran, Founder of the Blue Mountain Center of Meditation, reprinted by permission of Nilgiri Press, PO Box 256, Tomales, CA 94971.

Book design by Sharon Adams
Cover design by Leah Lococo

Library of Congress Cataloging-in-Publication Data

Names: Smith, Luther E., Jr., 1947– author.
Title: Hope is here! : spiritual practices for pursuing justice and beloved community / Luther E. Smith, Jr.
Description: First edition. | Louisville, Kentucky : Westminster John Knox Press, [2023] | Includes bibliographical references. | Summary: "Guides readers to perceive hope in all circumstances and in five spiritual practices that transform individuals, congregations, and society for justice and beloved community"— Provided by publisher.
Identifiers: LCCN 2023035003 (print) | LCCN 2023035004 (ebook) | ISBN 9780664268305 (paperback) | ISBN 9781646983636 (ebook)
Subjects: LCSH: Hope—Religious aspects—Christianity. | Christian life.
Classification: LCC BV4638 .S575 2023 (print) | LCC BV4638 (ebook) | DDC 234/.25—dc23/eng/20230927
LC record available at https://lccn.loc.gov/2023035003
LC ebook record available at https://lccn.loc.gov/2023035004

Most Westminster John Knox Press books are available at special quantity discounts when purchased in bulk by corporations, organizations, and special-interest groups. For more information, please e-mail SpecialSales@wjkbooks.com.

To Helen
Who embodies hope.

Contents

Preface

My father was intrigued by a sermon that invited him to reconsider the conclusions of a favorite Scripture (1 Cor. 13). He said the preacher described current traumas, fears, and anxieties that pervaded the country and world. He then affirmed the apostle Paul's naming of faith, hope, and love as abiding virtues, but instead of agreeing with Paul about the superiority of love, the preacher proposed that for current times the "greatest of these is *hope*." The preacher's conclusion startled my father and me. I had never heard anyone elevate hope to such heights. The spotlight on hope captured my attention, and I have never withdrawn my gaze. My journey with hope began anew and with regard for its "greatness." Assessing whether hope or love is greater has never been my aim. Understanding the significance, power, and ways of hope, however, became a spiritual quest that has disclosed hope's presence for all the seasons of my life.

In conversations, community meetings, media interviews, and books, I am attuned to the various ways hope is the emotion that I hear spoken about most often. Hope is used to speak to all matters of desire, optimism, and need. Whether used in relation to personal crises, anguish about loved ones, wanted or unwanted job transitions, foreboding weather forecasts, fanatic devotion to sports teams, threats to the soul of the nation, or horrors from international conflicts, the word "hope" announces our hearts' yearnings.

Still, I feel that the greatness of hope is rarely evident in how persons refer to it. Most often, I hear people speak of hope only as an optimistic feeling for an outcome they desire ("I have hope that the war will soon end") or as motivation for pursuing a goal ("Because my hope to succeed is so strong, I'll eventually find the right job"). Hope is considered an uplifting emotion to help us meet challenges near and far. In these expressions about hope, the greatness of hope is reduced. We settle for a domesticated version of hope that serves our desires.

In my journey with hope, I've wondered why hope was primarily seen as an emotional servant for feeling better. I have come to understand that the greatness of hope comes not when we treat it as a possession, but when we are *possessed by hope.*

Hope Is Here! offers readers insights and practices for nurturing a deeper relationship with hope. Yes, hope uplifts—*and does so much more.* Hope reveals, empowers, challenges, disrupts, transforms, and enlivens us to God's desire for our lives and the world. Readers will perceive hope in new ways and be invited to join the "work of hope" in their lives and in God's dream of beloved community. The spiritual journey with hope deepens our self-awareness, our interactions in relationships, and our involvement in social realities. All these places (self, relationships, society) disclose God's heart. We meet God and hope anew in these places; and we then become new to express our true selves, to nurture our relationships, and to contribute to healing the world.

Hope enables us to be alive and responsive to the wonders of each day. Hope sustains us through times we welcome and times that trouble us. Hope reveals to us opportunities to experience fulfillment. Hope inspires us to love with our whole being. Hope transforms us and the world for beloved community. The greatness of hope is here for us to pursue and know.

Christians committed to follow in the Way of Jesus are the primary audience for my writing. This includes Christians active in various church traditions; Christians who self identify as "spiritual but not religious"; Christians who are not involved in justice movements; and Christians whose social activism is rooted deeply in their faith. Common to all Christians is the need to journey with hope. Whatever the ordeals, joys, and heartbreaks on the journey, hope empowers Christian disciples to be steadfast in their commitment to journey with God. We must therefore be determined to perceive the profound meaning and work of hope. Otherwise, we may find ourselves failing to recognize how hope is already with us and transforming us.

The significance and power of hope is not exclusive to one religion. God's dream of beloved community resides with people from many faith traditions. My focus on Christians is to write from the tradition in which I am rooted. The Christian faith is my religious home. As a member of the Christian family, I write with gratitude for the inspiration, guidance, and spiritual formation given by our traditions. I offer my voice to proclaim how hope is so much more than our desires or feelings of optimism. Hope brings forth vitality that is salvific (healing and making whole) for us.

The Christian story portrays faithfulness to God's dream of beloved community. When fully told, the Christian story also has embarrassing betrayals of God's dream. Both the portrayals and betrayals are our heritage. *Hope Is Here!* focuses on how embracing hope is essential for disciples of Jesus to portray faithfulness to God. How might our faith witness, in this season, be a joy to God's heart? How might our discipleship contribute to a world that reflects God's dream? *Hope Is Here!* offers ways for us to answer these questions with our lives.

The book's subtitle, *Spiritual Practices for Pursuing Justice and Beloved Community*, indicates the fundamental role of spiritual practices to help persons deepen their sense of self and the sacred meaning of their work for justice and beloved community. Personal spiritual formation is vital to prepare and sustain us for being compassionate in relationships and persistent in social transformation. And our involvement in social change is crucial to both initiating and continuing personal spiritual growth. *Efforts in personal and congregational spiritual growth are deficient if they fail to advocate for social justice and compassion.* Oppressive social realities are where God's aching heart calls us to "do justice." Hope enlivens us to our capacities to affect personal and social transformations that delight God.

Spiritual practices are the disciplines (things to do) that instruct and deepen us in faith. Practices are more than concepts to read about as dimensions of faith. Spiritual practices are to faith what physical exercise is to health. Reading about walking does not replace the need to walk. The same is true for reading about spiritual practices.

The practices are behaviors *we enact* in our lives to empower our faith journey. Others can inspire us by demonstrating a practice; however, their example does not replace our need (our opportunity) to be practitioners.

A final comment about the subtitle. Justice is integral to beloved community. You may ask: "Why refer to justice *and* beloved community in the subtitle and throughout the book? I accentuate justice because people frequently do not associate justice with beloved community. Even though Dr. Martin Luther King Jr. referred to beloved community as a place and time where justice reigns, others often speak of beloved community only in terms of compassion, reconciliation, and harmony. Regarding justice apart from beloved community is analogous to writers who neglect justice when they focus on love or peace or reconciliation. This can leave the impression that love, peace, and reconciliation do not entail justice. In *Hope Is Here!*, whenever beloved community is discussed, it *always* includes justice. I often use the two terms together to avoid having justice forgotten while discussing beloved community.

In *Hope Is Here!* readers will encounter the immediacy and power of hope in many ways—including Scripture, stories, the persons interviewed for the book, my personal experiences, the spiritual practices, and their own lives. Whether you are reading the book alone or in a study group or for a class, responding to the book's questions will help you engage the significance of hope and the spiritual practices for your spiritual journey. I suggest that you write your responses in a journal or in this book for your ongoing reflection. Writing a response is often more engaging for reflection than trying to recall, perhaps days later, how you thought about a matter when you were reading.

Readers will sometimes review a book's table of contents and skip to a chapter that grabs their attention. I suggest that you avoid that approach in *Hope Is Here!* Each chapter builds upon and refers to preceding chapters. Reading the chapters sequentially will prove clearer for engaging hope and the spiritual practices.

The persons interviewed for this book are witnesses and contributors to the powerful work of hope. The Rev. Brian Combs, Ms. Fakhria Hussain Goksu, Ms. Taylor Emmaus McGhee, Bishop Marvin Frank Thomas Sr., and the Rev. Janet Wolf have been generous with their time and open hearts in describing their journeys. They inspire me. We are privileged to have their inspiring, transformational, and sacred stories for our journey in *Hope Is Here!*

Writers will attest that the merits of a manuscript do not assure its publication. I am grateful to Robert Ratcliff, editor of Westminster John Knox Press, who saw the promise of this book, encouraged its publication, and contributed to the many phases of its preparation. I also cherish the skilled involvement of Leslie Garrote, José Santana, Julie Tonini, Hermann Weinlick, Bridgett Green, Leah Lococo, Allison Taylor, and others who helped with the publication of this book.

Joy Borra's friendship, journalistic skills, and commitment to beloved community led her to agree to read and reread the manuscript. Her questions, affirmations, and editorial suggestions helped the writing be a conversation with readers. My gratitude exceeds expression.

My wife, Helen Pearson Smith, to whom this book is dedicated, lovingly insisted long ago that this understanding of hope was a sacred offering that is needed in our efforts to be a people for beloved community. She has been an advocate for the book and for readers pursuing hope. When my other writing projects concluded, Helen persisted in reminding me that writing this book on hope was a calling. I am grateful for her encouragement, the many conversations on the book's themes, editorial suggestions, and companionship on the journey with hope.

All those acknowledged for helping me on the journey with hope await your joining us to pursue the greatness of hope. Together, we will not exhaust hope's significance, but we can perceive and bear testimony to its presence and power in ways we had not known previously. Perhaps the transformative work of hope has brought us together on this journey so that we might discover what hope seeks to accomplish through us and for us. I welcome our discernment and witnessing to the greatness of hope in our lives.

Luther E. Smith Jr.
Stone Mountain, Georgia

Chapter One

Where Hope Abides

It may be that the only clue to the eternal available to us
is found in the tight circle of time and space
by which our little lives are grounded and defined.
—Howard Thurman, *With Head and Heart*

Something is loosed to change the shaken world,
And with it we must change!
—Stephen Vincent Benét, *A Child Is Born:*
A Modern Drama of the Nativity

Hope Is

Hope is here! With us now! Available for the transformations needed in the world and in our personal lives! Hope is not waiting for miracle medications or changes in political leadership. Its presence is not dependent upon eliminating racism or treaties ending conflicts. As poverty and injustice persist, hope remains. Hope refuses to abandon us, though despairing conditions prevail both externally and within our hearts. Hope abides with us and is active in our immediate realities—whatever they may be. Understanding this everpresent nature and transformative power of hope can relieve our feeling forlorn in troubling times. Hope is here to empower us to live life more fully.

Perceiving hope as always with us is neither Pollyannaish nor a rejection of living with painful outcomes. Hope does not rely on illusions about reality and our capacities. Hope is strong, persevering, and here for us *now*. If we embrace its true nature and purpose, we need not live with illusory understandings of hope. This chapter reveals hope's immediacy and transformative power, not just for our circumstances, but *for us!* Contrary to our understanding of hope only as an attitude (hopefulness) or as a source that lifts our spirits as we anticipate fulfillment of desires, hope often *disrupts* our desires. This difference is consequential.

Aligning our faith commitment with God's hope for us is essential to perceiving the immediacy of hope for personal transformation and for beloved community. Our faith journey requires compelling visions of beloved community that God dreams for us—visions that depict the essence and work of hope. Becoming a people of hope involves paying attention to the visions and the lens through which we perceive the visions. Our faith journey also involves opening our hearts to the spiritual practices that help forge our becoming. The chapter and its questions summon more than intriguing considerations about hope; they summon decisions for living as a testimony to hope.

"Hope" is one of the most treasured words to express the hunger of the heart. We hope that our health and the health of those we love are strong in sustaining us for the adventure of life. We hope our children will flourish. We hope to be successful in the work that gives us joy. We hope that compassion and justice prevail in our homeland and throughout the world. In these ways, hope is the heart's *desire*.

"Hope" is also used for what is thought to be *a trustworthy source* for a desired outcome: "Without question I place hope in our governmental institutions to withstand any assault on our democracy." "I know we will recover from the flood damage because I have hope in the goodness and responsiveness of people." In these examples, "hope" identifies sources that we believe have the power to answer perceived threats and devastating circumstances.

Even when the word "hope" is not used, it is implied when persons speak their *expectations* that a particular time and/or set of circumstances will birth new realities into their lives. This is captured in the religious proclamation of God's impending action in history: "When the Messiah comes . . ." During the 1960s, I often heard social activists declare their anticipation that injustices would be reversed, "When the revolution comes . . ." When scientists lack explanations for the questions that arise from their experiments, many speak their hope that future scientific investigation will yield the breakthroughs that now elude their efforts. When needed social change seems destined to be deferred beyond our lifetime, persons will often say, "The next generation will bring new attitudes and energies to moving society in the right direction." Hope is envisioned in the tomorrows that hold the promise for what we so hunger to receive today.

Hope as desire, trustworthy sources for our desires, and anticipating a promising future are the most familiar ways we use the word. Using "hope" in these ways not only names what we want, how we feel, and what we believe; it also fashions our commitments of time, energy, and resources. As with many words, "hope" has various meanings for speaking our hearts. However, if we interpret hope *only* in terms of longing, conviction, and anticipation, we most likely end up knowing more about ourselves than we do about the fullness of hope. It's crucial that we discover a more expansive and sacred meaning of hope.

Likewise, although we often speak of "love" in terms of personal feelings, love is more than feelings of affection. Love compels caring, even when we do not feel affectionate toward another. When Jesus instructed, "Love your enemies" (Matt. 5:44), he called us to relate with love, even though we suffer our enemies' abuses. Also, we can experience love from others even when we do not feel loved. However intense our passion for someone or something, our feelings and behaviors do not exhaust the power and meaning of love. We must take care to avoid domesticating love and hope as only human emotions. *Love and hope are God's essential transformative forces for beloved community.* A community based on hope requires love, and a community based on love requires hope.

Perceiving hope as *a transformative force* is fundamental to perceiving "the greatness of hope" discussed in the preface. We do not experience hope because we have intensified our efforts to be optimistic or gathered more resources to address our problems. These initiatives may result in our *feeling hopeful*, but the purpose and work of hope are not obliged to conform to whatever we select to feel encouraged about. We experience hope because *hope possesses us* on its terms. Grasping this meaning of hope is crucial to our journey in this and forthcoming chapters.

I proffer two approaches for opening minds and hearts to this understanding of hope as purposeful and immediate. (1) Relax and possibly release the effort to make hope captive to what you want it to be. The faith journey is taken to see even unexpected disclosures of God's love and ways. (2) Trust the spiritual practices to guide your ongoing formation for God's sake. The greatness of hope far exceeds our desires, trustworthy sources for our desires, and our anticipating a promising future. *Hope Is Here!* invites us to recognize and respond to hope as a force of God that enlivens us to life.

A Force of God That Enlivens Us to Life

God is not estranged from creation—including each one of us. Even indifference to God and corrupt behaviors do not cause God to abandon us. The prophet Jeremiah pleads, "Although our iniquities testify against us . . . [and] our rebellions indeed are many, and we have sinned against you. . . . Yet you, O LORD, are in the midst of us, and we are called by your name; do not forsake us" (Jer. 14:7, 9b). The apostle Paul writes to assure Christians in Rome that whatever their challenges, God sustains them. His confidence about God's everlasting love is expressed through his Christ-centered theology: "For I am convinced that neither death, nor life, nor angels, nor rulers, nor things present, nor things to come, nor powers, nor height, nor depth, nor anything else in all creation will be able to separate us from the love of God in Christ Jesus our Lord" (Rom. 8:38–39).

Throughout the Christian Scriptures, God's covenantal relationship with humanity is sealed by God's love. God's judgments and blessings come from God's loving responsiveness.

> Your steadfast love, O LORD, extends to the heavens,
>   your faithfulness to the clouds.
> Your righteousness is like the mighty mountains;
>   your judgments are like the great deep;
>   you save humans and animals alike, O LORD.

How precious is your steadfast love, O God!
All people may take refuge in the shadow of your wings.

(Ps. 36:5–7)

Steadfast love is a sustaining and transforming force of God. Wherever God is, love is. Wherever God's love is, hope is. *Love and hope are inseparable forces of God.* Speak about one at any length, and your description will sound increasingly like the other. Beware of any situation where one of these forces is claimed to be operative without the other. Actions in such a situation may be done in the name of God, but they are not of God.

Beating a child to correct insolent behavior may be motivated by a parent's determination to prevent increasing acts of disrespect that will be ruinous for the child's future. However well intended is the punishment to preserve a bright future for the child, the beating will likely be experienced as a traumatizing and alienating act of dominance. Mass incarceration results from promises to the public that a less crime-ridden future will come when those convicted are held in jails and prisons. However, mass incarceration is a strategy that fails to consider how lengthy prison sentences, prison conditions, and the elimination of rehabilitation programs are damaging to the incarcerated, their families, their communities, and the larger society. Proposed tax cuts that leave families and corporations with more disposable income can appear to be policy that brings increased financial vitality to a community. However, when those same tax cuts jeopardize funding the social safety nets for people living in poverty, the whole proposal becomes cruelty. A vision of hope that excludes compassion for all involved is a charade. Any future worth anticipating as an expression of hope requires love.

With hope and love identified as forces of God, expect to hear, "But what if someone does not believe in God?" "Do atheists have hope?" "What about agnostics?" To be clear, the reality of hope is not dependent on believing in God. By analogy, the reality of gravity is not dependent upon believing in it. Some people base their understanding of hope on science or human ingenuity or moral rectitude. Their beliefs do not nullify the reality of God or the presence of hope as a force for their lives. Hope is an equal-opportunity force. The challenge for each person is to discern hope correctly and to live with a vitality that feeds the hunger of the heart. My personal and ancestral testimony about hope is grounded in God.

⚜ ⚜ ⚜ ⚜ ⚜ ⚜ ⚜

Hope is purposeful. As a force of God, it enlivens us to life. Acting upon and within us, hope inspires us to imagine creatively, perceive reality anew, persevere in despair, risk with opportunities, and trust beyond our control. Hope exists with the purpose of expanding our awareness and hearts to experience God's abiding love through all creation—including ourselves. When catastrophes wreak havoc upon the land, hope works to cause us to lament and to repair the damage. When personal trauma feels like more than the human spirit can bear, hope works to strengthen resolve and to bring the desolate into the company of healing relationships. Even when the manifestation of hope we most desire does not occur, hope engages us to endure . . . or to marshal our strength to pursue creative next steps . . . or to understand ourselves and our challenges more clearly than before. *Hope emboldens us to give ourselves for a future worth anticipating.* More of ourselves is available to take the next step with an increased sense of capacity for what is daunting or promising or both.

Physical pain can literally stop us from taking "the next step." Pain not only controls movement; pain also commands our full attention. What's wrong? What caused this? Was this a momentary hurt or a signal of more to come? Will the trouble heal itself, or do I need a medical examination? What medicine will address lingering discomfort? Should I seek something or someone to assure this will not happen again? Pain triggers anxiety and fear—emotions that construe hope as eliminating the pain.

Chronic pain is a whole other magnitude of severity. No timetable exists for pain relief. It can overwhelm our physical and emotional energy to endure and be available to what gives us joy. What troubles today is foreseen as the experience in all our tomorrows. Facing the dire outlook for the future, the pain of the present moment intensifies. Chronic pain not only consumes our energy; it alters our relationships with persons, our vocations, our dreams, and our sense of self. Hope's work in these varied experiences is to bring forth vitality and joy to purposeful living. Its impact is personal and communal as it abides with sufferers, supporters, medical professionals, and those reticent to become involved. Hope persists to birth us anew.

Reynolds Price gives testimony to this in his memoir, *A Whole New Life*. His chronic pain began in his early fifties when he was already an acclaimed novelist, playwright, essayist, poet, and professor. A cancerous tumor in his spinal cord caused excruciating pain and treatments that resulted in the paralysis of his legs. The extent of his pain was so severe on one day, that when asked to indicate his pain level on a scale from one to ten ("*ten* being agony to the point of unconsciousness"), he responded "twelve." Price remained in pain for the rest of his life and never walked again.

The memoir is uncompromising in portraying the shock of the life-changing assault on his body (both by the tumor and medical treatments), emotional distress, and the death of whom he had known himself to be. With his remarkable writing, we understand the horror of the long and traumatic struggle. After bearing witness to this struggle, he writes:

> I think I can say that almost any degree of physical pain can be borne. And not only borne but literally displaced from the actual center of a human life and then ignored. I can make that claim because I'm convinced that all pain has one huge design on us—to rule our minds—and therefore that the secret of living with pain is wanting hard to throw it out of central control, then finding the sane means to work that steady mental combination of distancing and coexistence.[1]

Pain continued to be felt. But pain was not in control of who he was and who he was becoming. Explaining how he endured and advanced not only to "a whole new life," but also to "a better life," he writes that among "the first props beneath my own collapse" was prayer.[2] Especially noted are prayers spoken from the depths of agony about what would come next, and the answer he received was "more." In the depths, this is not the response one longs to hear. Price, however, received the answer as the assurance of God's presence and as the caring alert to prepare. Speaking gratitude for all who sustained him through his ordeal, he includes, "The unseen hand of the source of all has never felt absent as long as a week."[3]

Forever in pain, forever a paraplegic, he speaks about being a more sensitive person to what most counts in life, to having "work sent by God" that has enabled him to be more productive and having more delight with friends and students. This is no glorification of pain. It is, rather, a testimony about what can be done with pain so that it does not capture one and prevent one from being enlivened to life. Excluding the four years of trial and error of his most intense suffering, he writes, *"I've yet to watch another life that seems to have brought more pleasure to its owner than mine has to me."* [4]

Richard M. Cohen's *Strong at the Broken Places: Voices of Illness, a Chorus of Hope* pursues the meaning of hope for persons with chronic illness. Cohen's life struggles with multiple sclerosis and colon cancer explain his motivation for the book: "I had embarked on a journey to see chronic illness through lenses other than my own."[5] Over a period of two years, he cultivated relationships with five persons, each with a life-changing illness: ALS (amyotrophic lateral sclerosis, also known as Lou Gehrig's disease); non-Hodgkin's lymphoma; Duchenne muscular dystrophy; Crohn's disease; and bipolar disorder. Their journeys are as varied as their diseases, backgrounds, personalities, and support systems. Still, common is their hunger to live with hope. Cohen makes clear that their hope is not expressed as anticipating a medical cure. They want to know themselves and to be known as more than their diseases. This involves living with a sense of purpose that makes a difference in their lives and the lives of others: experiencing loving relationships and community, having enjoyable moments, having a sense of agency about how to live.

Explicit references to God vary. As I said earlier, "the reality of hope is not dependent on believing in God. . . . Hope is an equal-opportunity force." While many may look inward or to relationships, the religious utilize prayer to announce to God, "I am here!" The announcing declares our readiness for God's enlivening power so that we can experience the fullness of life.

Reynolds Price and Richard Cohen bear testimony that even chronic illness and pain do not defeat the enlivening power of hope. Hope that is only "desire" does not survive unrelenting pain. Soon or late, when the permanence of illness and pain is undeniable, hope based completely on emotions of desire or the eventual removal of pain will not prevail. However, the testimonies of Price and Cohen portray the greatness of hope as an enlivening force even when suffering continues. We are wise to remember their witness to the enduring power of hope when our own lives confront pain and suffering. Their examples can inspire and assure that even in affliction and tribulation, hope does not abandon us.

⚜ ⚜ ⚜ ⚜ ⚜ ⚜ ⚜

The personal examples for living creatively with pain and disease have implications for chronic communal anguish. We are more than our social illnesses, and it's essential that we do not concede our destinies to their damaging power. *Commitment to our God-given sense of purpose must be as relentless as the pain.* Joyful times can and must be experienced even as pain persists. We have agency in being enlivened to life.

Our communities suffer from systemic racism, environmental hazards, mass incarceration, deadly poverty, chemical addiction, domestic abuse, gun violence, and a legion of other ills. Some people feel the pain of these ills more than others. They struggle daily to breathe freely in suffocating circumstances. What feels unbearable today has no sign of diminishing in all their tomorrows. The intense pain is theirs; the deadly sicknesses affect *everyone.*

Even if the commitment to justice and beloved community is not the motivation of everyone, indifference to the crises of communal pain is unacceptable. People primarily motivated by self-interest ought to understand that the named diseases of society are malignant. They affect some directly and all indirectly. Unless we engage these ills, they will destroy lives, public institutions, and social ideals for generations.

As an allegory, imagine society as occupying a high-rise building. The basement and lower levels are where the poor and oppressed are confined to live by virtue of their limited resources and the long-standing codes of the building. The most affluent have penthouses on the top floors. Everyone else lives on the middle floors. When a fire starts in the basement and begins to move up one level after another, residents on the upper floors may be concerned, but the distance between them and the fire leads them to conclude that no crisis exists.

They return to whatever had their attention before the fire began. It's difficult for them to believe that what is happening to those near the ground could endanger their well-being. Their privilege has led them to assume that their building's state-of-the-art fire-extinguishing system, the history of firefighters rushing to their rescue, and the privileges that come with occupying the upper floors will protect them from the fire with which the less fortunate are contending.

You see where this is going. Just having sympathy for those on the lower levels will not be life-giving for anyone. Persons living on the upper levels who feel no sense of obligation to address the crises occurring to those living below them are naive and hard-hearted. Middle and upper tenants would be foolish to believe that the fire cannot reach them. Yet the world house burns as if no crisis exists. If you think this allegory oversimplifies social stratification and crises, I agree with you. But that does not make it inaccurate. Those above the lower levels may not have set the fire; previous generations may be responsible. Nevertheless, indifference allows the fire to rage.

Becoming a people for justice and beloved community involves becoming *engaged* in the healing process. Indifference is not a faithful option. Love and hope provide the strength and courage to be present to pain and to focus energies on the work God dreams for us. Pain will continue, but we will experience *a whole new life*.

Fulfilling God's dream for us is hope's purpose. The biblical narrative of God's dream for us can be interpreted as our becoming a people enlivened to God's will that love and justice prevail in us, in our relationships, and throughout creation. Hope empowers the realization of this dream. Hope is an unrelenting force that is not destroyed, even in the midst of pain, carnage, and defeat. As God persists, hope persists.

On the social level, the reality of hope as a purposeful force is evident in the speeches of Martin Luther King Jr. when he assured his listeners that though the civil rights struggle was protracted and difficult, the outcome of the struggle was certain. He often quoted theologian and social reformer Theodore Parker, who said, "The arc of the moral universe is long, but it bends toward justice." In other words, life-affirming energies are embedded in the very structure of existence. This conviction is heard from Archbishop Desmond Tutu, who, while living under the oppressive apartheid system of South Africa, declared, "Apartheid is already dead." He described their current crisis as fueled by guardians of apartheid who failed to accept that they were frantically trying to sustain a system that had no future. Apartheid contradicted the creative energies of life that reflect God's will for humanity. In essence, the fate of apartheid was doomed before it was even established. Purposeful forces are at work in life to resist injustice and despair, and to empower compassion and creativity. Hope is such a force.

Becoming a People of Hope for Beloved Community

"Beloved community" is a term that characterizes God's dream for us. Martin Luther King Jr. used this term for casting his vision of community based on love, respect, justice, reconciliation, and nonviolent protest. King was indebted to Josiah Royce (1855–1916), who coined the term "beloved community" to emphasize the fundamental role of community in shaping moral persons. Both Royce and King perceived community as the crucible for forming moral persons who contribute to the commonweal.

Biblical images symbolizing beloved community abound:

> They shall beat their swords into plowshares,
>   and their spears into pruning hooks;
> nation shall not lift up sword against nation;
>   neither shall they learn war any more.
>   (Isa. 2:4)

> The wolf shall live with the lamb;
>   the leopard shall lie down with the kid;
> the calf and the lion will feed together,
>   and a little child shall lead them.
>   (Isa. 11:6)

> Give justice to the weak and the orphan;
>   maintain the right of the lowly and the destitute.
> Rescue the weak and the needy;
>   deliver them from the hand of the wicked.
>   (Ps. 82:3–4)

All who believed were together and had all things in common; they would sell their possessions and goods and distribute the proceeds to all, as any had need. Day by day, as they spent much time together in the temple, they broke bread at home and ate their food with glad and generous hearts, praising God and having the goodwill of all the people. (Acts 2:44–47)

The prophet Micah summarizes what God requires of us personally and collectively: "to do justice and to love kindness and to walk humbly with your God" (Mic. 6:8). When asked about the greatest commandment, Jesus responds: "'You shall love the Lord your God with all your heart and with all your soul and with all your mind.' This is the greatest and first commandment. And a second is like it: 'You shall love your neighbor as yourself'" (Matt. 22:37–39). Later, Jesus describes love as caring for those who are hungry and thirsty, strangers, naked, sick, and in prison (Matt. 25:31–46). These Scriptures inspire visions that animate our becoming a people for beloved community. Hope enlivened these faith ancestors to see the vision of community God dreams.

Martin Luther King Jr. cast a vision in his "I Have a Dream" speech at the 1963 March on Washington for Jobs and Freedom. In addition to inspiring King's prophetic witness, this vision ("dream") inspired and continues to inspire masses of people in the struggle for justice and equality. We not only have the images and testimonies of these ancestors; we also have the need and responsibility to cast our visions of beloved community that arise from perceiving God's dream for *our* lives, visions of beloved community that depict the essence and work of hope. Without a compelling vision, our faith journey is prone to be consumed by myriad matters that continually clamor for our attention and time; or we wander indecisively among competing ideologies. Visions of beloved community inspire us to persist with a sacred purpose when present realities fail to reflect who God intends us to be for one another.

Coming to agreement about the work of hope and a vision of beloved community can be difficult. Each of us has lived with hope. Our individual understandings of the abiding presence of hope, however, are often at odds with one another. Even when persons experience the same situations, they often have contrasting feelings and interpretations about what has occurred. A friend and I go to a movie. She leaves depressed because the heroic character is killed by repressive authorities. I leave inspired because of the resoluteness and courage of the hero. She experiences futility; I experience hope. Our life experiences shape *the interpretive lens* we wear in seeing reality.

Becoming a people of hope involves paying attention to the interpretive lens. We are wise to reflect on the experiences that have shaped our lens; and we need to discern when these experiences bring focus and when they distort. Reality is determined not only by what our eyes behold in the world, but also by the lens through which our hearts perceive.

I offer a sketch of my interpretive lens. I've grown up as a Black male in the United States. My parents and sister created a home with abundant love, laughter, affirmation, and all that could be desired from a nurturing family. My local Methodist church was my second family. When I thought about misbehaving, I worried about disappointing those at the church as much as I did my parents. Worship services, especially the music, thrilled and transported my spirit to timeless realms that assured me for all time.

At age five I had already experienced discrimination in a downtown department store that refused lunch-counter food service to African Americans—an incident that pained my mother as she explained why we could not eat there. As a five-year old I watched presidential conventions and had a fervent desire for my candidate, Adlai Stevenson, to win, because he had expressed a stronger commitment to civil rights for Black people. When I was eight years old, I saw, and can still see, the monstrous face of Emmett Till in *Jet Magazine* after he had been brutalized, murdered, and drowned by White racists in Money, Mississippi. The message was sent about what would occur to even a child if White people felt insulted. In school I had many classroom drills on what we should do in case of a nuclear attack. As a teenager waiting on a bus, I suffered the humiliation of having the police require me to face and lean against a wall with my hands raised as they searched me and questioned me because I "looked like someone who was reported to them." At age seventy-one, while walking near the hotel where I stayed as a guest university lecturer, I was stopped and questioned by a police officer because a nearby bank was uncomfortable with my walking near it.

I've worked as a community organizer to empower welfare recipients to receive their benefits. While I was doing this work, I had death threats and my car was firebombed. Courageous activists have fueled my passion for justice. My teachers and students have taught me lessons and questions to be lived beyond the classroom. Friends and family members have been constant in their outpouring of love. Friends and family members have been killed by gun violence. Wave after wave of national crises have landed on my heart—the civil rights struggle and the assassinations of its leaders, the Vietnam war, women denied equal rights and pay, the United States government's reticence to condemn apartheid in South Africa, mass incarceration, September 11, the defamation of Jews and Muslims, discrimination and violence against persons because of their sexual orientation, the demonization of immigrants and refugees, a pandemic, and an insurrection targeting the US Capitol. This is but a thumbnail sketch of formative experiences that have shaped the interpretive lens through which I see reality.

In addition, my life journey with hope also includes journeying with formative ancestors. Ancestors in Africa. Ancestors in slavery. Ancestors who gave everything in the fight for freedom. Ancestors who bore witness to hope amid despairing realities. Their story is my story. They are in my "cloud of witnesses"; their lives bear testimony to hope as a force of God that enlivens us to life. Their lives instruct me on becoming a person for justice and beloved community.

What seminal life experiences have informed your outlook on hope and beloved community? How do they shape your lens? How do you interpret the work of hope in your life? Avoid selecting only experiences of relief and joy. Identify times when the cry for healing seemed unheard or ignored or muffled. Who are formative ancestors for you and for your understanding of hope?

Hope and Hopefulness

The difference between hope and hopefulness is consequential. As I previously stated, the word "hope" is used frequently to express "desire, to name trustworthy sources for our desires, and anticipating a promising future." These understandings of hope are appealing, because the fulfillment of our desires could result in so much good. We desire healing, peace, acceptance, and other outcomes that bring us joy. To hope is to believe in the fulfillment of the heart's longings. *We often experience a reassuring agreement between our desires and hope's mission to enliven us to life.* Often, but not always. We are prone to be hopeful (i.e., to desire and expect) about much that is not worthy of us. Choose any of the "deadly sins." People long to make headlines with greed, wrath, envy, or lust. We are capable of desiring to be lost or dead to the moral world. With zeal we calculate for our "advantage," regardless of the cost to our spirits or the community.

For most of us, while our desires are not so blatantly corrupt, they are frequently captive to self-interest. My desires are strongest for my ambitions, my career, my family, my friends, my people. This concern for one's own is natural and often positive. It reflects the heart's commitment to vocation and intimate relationships—a commitment that contributes to the creative impulse of life. However, I must always be careful not to assume that what I want, as noble and laudable as it may be, is what God wants. God's heart embraces much that I fear, hate, ignore, and reject. This challenges the presumption that my desires are what God desires for the work of hope.

Although we are likely to continue using the word "hope" as an expression of our desires, hope itself is more than personal desire. Otherwise, we misunderstand the very essence of hope as God's enlivening force for all. God desires to save the world—the very world with needs that can intimidate our feelings of hopefulness. So many interests in this world compete with our self-interest. We can find ourselves adamant about our desires and less responsive to God's desires. We wonder if God's passion for the world takes into account our fragility and our dreams. Our hopefulness may be at odds with hope as a force of God. The problem is not with God, or even the desires of others we deem threatening. The problem is with us. We need our desiring to be made right. This too is the work of hope. Rather than being a servant to our desires, the force of hope tutors our desiring. Rather than fulfilling our wishes, hope makes demands of us. Rather than having what we desire brought to us, hope takes us to where we might come alive. Hope enlivens us through experiences that tutor our hopefulness.

Being hopeful is a hunger of the heart. We yearn for the next moment or coming years to free us from oppression. We long for possibilities that transform anguish to joy, war to peace, injury to healing, pain to comfort, hatred to love, injustice and alienation to beloved community. Psalm 40 epitomizes this personal "cry" for deliverance from deadly existence:

> I waited patiently for the LORD;
>   he inclined to me and heard my cry.
> He drew me up from the desolate pit,
>   out of the miry bog,
> and set my feet upon a rock,
>   making my steps secure.
> He put a new song in my mouth,
>   a song of praise to our God.
>   (Ps. 40:1–3)

Here waiting refers to the time between experiences of desolation and rescue; it is not a theological assertion of God's absence. The psalmist is able to wait patiently, with the emotion of hopefulness, because of the assurance that God can be trusted to be present. The Negro spiritual "Hold On (Just a Little While Longer)," sung in the desolate circumstances of slavery, testifies about the power of waiting for a hopeful outcome. The title is also the song's constant refrain. Two verses change "hold on" to "pray on" and then "sing on." Waiting is active. There are empowering ways to wait. Each verse concludes with the sung assurance that "everything will be alright."

Again, the distinction between hope and hopefulness is consequential. Hope is always present, because God is always present. Hope is with us, even when we do not feel hopeful. It's crucial to know how to live creatively, how to live as people for beloved community, even when we do not feel hopeful. Restoring our hearts in the assurance that hope is here, despite travails, can be comforting and energizing. We are not abandoned. We are not bereft of enlivening possibility.

Those whose lives witness to the power of hope demonstrate that the human spirit can endure the most horrific circumstances of life . . . except possibly the protracted feeling of utter abandonment.

Unrelenting pain, imprisonment, slavery, the traumas of war, depression, betrayal, and deep grief shake the foundations of our very being. The resulting despair may be not only a first reaction but also a final one. Death may be chosen over the will to live. Still, the record of history is replete with the testimonies of persons who came to a greater embrace of life despite their horrific experiences. They connected with a force within and external to themselves that sustained them, even when they were not hopeful. Feeling alone, isolated, overwhelmed, depleted? Yes. But also sensing, perhaps below conscious awareness, that they were not *utterly* abandoned. Hope can sustain even when one does not feel hopeful.

Reassurance and sustenance come from knowing *hope is here.* In addition, especially in circumstances of distress, the hunger of the heart for hopefulness must be fed. Faithful hopefulness is based on hope's mission to engage us with life so that we become *our true selves—the selves that God created us to be.* Our pursuit of joy must not be confined to a "safe" harbor constructed by anxieties, fears, and prejudices. The power of hope launches us beyond imprisoning realities and frees our senses to be enlivened by what we experience. Hopefulness occurs on this journey. Selves become openhearted to sorrow and care. Selves work through the conflicts and confusion entailed in living creatively with others. This book focuses on opportunities and practices for us to be enlivened by hope, to experience hopefulness, and to live as a people for justice and beloved community.

"I Will Sing a New Song"

Howard Thurman's meditation "I Will Sing a New Song" builds on the Psalm 40 phrase "He [God] put a new song in my mouth," which describes the creative response persons "must" make when previous understandings and efforts have proven deficient. In part it reads:

> I will sing a new song.
> I must learn the new song for the new needs.

I must fashion new words born of all the new growth
     of my life—of my mind—of my spirit.
I must prepare for new melodies that have
     never been mine before,
That all that is within me may lift my voice unto God.[6]

The meditation names a faithful response to hope—a response that births faithful hopefulness. Singing a new song is both a means to and a sign of personal transformation. Transformation to God-centered hopefulness and beloved community is hope's enlivening purpose.

An African adage declares, "Before the spirit can descend, a song must be sung." The power of song is professed as a means to be alive to the experience and purposes of the Divine. Whether we are alone, gathered in worship, or on a protest march, singing transforms and readies us to experience the enlivening spirit of God. Gloomy moods are brightened. Familiar songs become *new songs* when we sing with others to overcome injustice.

Even singing the "blues" as musical genre can be a means for affirming one's capacity to persevere. Heartbreaking loss? Yes. Denied every effort to work? Yes. Soul-crushing imprisonment? Yes. Yet in all this, one's voice is not muted. A person can sing. Singing itself becomes the bulwark against despair. In the song "Stormy Blues," Billie Holiday declares being so familiar with bad times that bad times are inconsequential. B. B. King brings forth laughter when he sings, "Nobody loves me but my mother, and she could be jivin' too." The singers are in a bad state of feeling and mind. Still, they are sustained and they endure by singing about their condition.

In *The Negro Spiritual Speaks of Life and Death,* Howard Thurman writes that enslaved African Americans created songs that professed hope in God and that enabled them to live with hopefulness despite the horrors of slavery. Thurman concludes that the singing of these songs is a profound demonstration of the human capacity to trust in God's prevailing love and comforting assurance. He assesses these captive singers to be among "the great religious thinkers of the human race. They made a worthless life, the life of chattel property, a mere thing, a body, *worth living!*"[7]

Singing that enlivens our spirits to endure, persist, rest assured, and rejoice is a spiritual practice for hopefulness and becoming a people for justice and beloved community. What songs do you sing through joyful and troubling times? The question is not asking, "Can you carry a tune?" but "Do you have a tune that carries you?" Hope feeds our insatiable hunger to sing a new song!

Singing, in addition to being a literal spiritual practice, has figurative significance. Singing can also refer to how the body is being given to harmonizing with what is vital in life. Like music, life is lived with a sense of tempos, tonalities, rhythms, and improvisations. Every day we compose our lives by how we live. Moods of happiness and despair, eagerness and boredom, love and indifference, courage and fear, celebration and grief inform how our whole bodies voice our dedication to "the art of living." Singing a new song is not just about the song. Primarily, the singing expresses that *we are becoming new*!

❖ ❖ ❖ ❖ ❖

Our becoming new may be experienced as hope coming forth from within us and/or coming to us from without. However, sustaining our hope-inspired formation, which includes our hopefulness, relies upon giving ourselves to practices (commonly called "disciplines" in the Christian spirituality literature) that align us with God's yearnings for us and the world. We have responsibility for our formation. And we have *response ability* for our formation. There are actions (practices/disciplines) we can take for our becoming a people of hope.

The necessity of personal action is evident in the Thurman meditation I quoted. He says, "I must learn the new song. . . . I must fashion new words. . . . I must prepare for new melodies." Practices help forge our becoming. Commitment to becoming a people for justice and beloved community involves being a people formed by the practices of hope.

The practices are experiences that reveal. They engage us with ourselves and with others beyond what we have known. The meaning of living with hope is deepened. Our hopefulness is nourished. We bring more wisdom to discerning among the paths forward. We live each day with greater assurance about "things we can do" to live fully.

Throughout history, spiritual practices have been deemed essential to spiritual formation and guidance. The number of ascetic practices is legion; fasting, self-imposed poverty, flagellation, wearing a hairshirt, and becoming a hermit are just a few examples. Even more numerous are the spiritual practices not based on experiencing severe physical and emotional pain; among the list of these types of practices are hospitality, meditation, giving alms, study, journaling, receiving spiritual direction, and worship. The five spiritual practices I identify in chapters 3–7 are not in the ascetic category. Still, their formative impact can lead to singing a new song that has been learned from welcomed and disruptive experiences of hope.

The spiritual practices are *contemplative praying, prophetic remembering, crossing identity boundaries, transforming conflict, and celebrating community.* Each of the five practices is available to us. We need not travel to a far country or encounter a spiritual mediator to be practitioners. The practices are also within our "response ability" to enact them in our lives. Each spiritual practice empowers personal and collective transformation for beloved community. The deepest understanding of the practices comes from experiencing their interrelatedness. *Hope is here in the spiritual practices!*

Questions for the Quest

"Journey" is frequently used to describe how one is living the spiritual life. It evokes images of movement, seeking, engaging new realities and new meanings, and risk. The journey is a quest. A quest inspired by hope. A quest to feed the spirit's hunger for fulfillment. A quest, whether or not we are aware of it, to give ourselves to God's dream of beloved community.

A journey's realities and our feelings about these realities are known and not known. Reliable maps? Maybe. Trustworthy testimony from previous travelers? Maybe. Support from others? Maybe. A strong desire to have a successful journey? Yes. Certainty that it will match our desire? No. Will I be safe? Maybe. Will I be the same at journey's end? No. Is there an end to the journey? Begin and see.

The questions evoke more questions. Even answers evoke more questions. Questions are not our nemesis. Certainty may be our downfall, but not questions. With questions we quest with a searching heart and a humility that are crucial to being alive to wisdom and confusion. The work of hope is accomplished with our embrace of the questions that inform and form us. I have previously written:

> In his "Introduction" to Pablo Neruda's *Book of Questions*, William O'Daly writes that "our greatest act of faith" may be "living in a state of visionary surrender to the elemental questions, free of the quiet desperation of clinging too tightly to answers."[8] Questions create a space-in-time for reflection. A question causes us to ponder all that informs the reason for the question. And when we confront something more significant than a rhetorical question, a question can cause us to pause and consider and reconsider a response—perhaps for the rest of our lives. Questions deepen our spirits to address the deep hunger.[9]

Questions are pivotal in Jesus' life and in our understanding him. When John the Baptist is on death row and is desperate to know if immediate hope is near for God's transforming movement, he tells his disciples to go to Jesus with the question, "Are you the one who is to come, or are we to expect someone else?" (Luke 7:19). Jesus is curious if his disciples, those closest to him, truly understand who he is, so he asks, "But who do you say that I am?" (Luke 9:20). A rich ruler is eager to know if his behavior is sufficient to receive an eternal reward, so he asks Jesus, "Good Teacher, what must I do to inherit eternal life?" (Luke 18:18). Dying on the cross, Jesus utters a question that comes from unimaginable suffering and an anguished heart: "My God, my God, why have you forsaken me?" (Mark 15:34). Questions abound on Jesus' spiritual journey. Disciples of Jesus are therefore wise to recognize the significance of questions in being on the quest with Jesus.

This book honors the role of questions for questing. In addition to questions asked throughout each chapter, a "Questing with Questions" section concludes each chapter. As an individual or in a study group, identify the questions that most capture your urge to reflect. Consider writing the thoughts and feelings that emerge—thoughts and feelings about the questions and/or your effort to respond to them. Linger with what you have written. Returning in days, months, or years to what you have written may be a time of reaffirming what stirred in you at the time of your first writing, or you may be surprised by how your reflections have changed. This can be a process where you encounter yourself as a mentor on the quest. *Hope is here in the questions!*

The immediacy of hope comes with the immediacy of a loving God. What a comforting assurance for living through life's personal and social vagaries. Whenever you declare, "I am here," you can give yourself to discerning how hope is here to tutor your hopefulness, enliven you through all circumstances, and prepare you to be a person for beloved community, as you sing a new song, are formed by spiritual practices, and quest with revealing questions.

Questing with Questions

1. How is hope endeavoring to enliven you to life?
2. Identify an event or period when you felt that you were experiencing beloved community. As you reflect upon it, what evoked the feeling of being in beloved community?
3. When have you been inspired to sing a new song? What occurred? How would you describe your new song? How have you sustained such singing? If you have not continued to sing it, why not?
4. What question(s) asked in the chapter connect with your questing heart? Reflect on why you have chosen the question(s).
5. What are your questions from reading this chapter?

Chapter Two

Hope's Work and Its Witnesses

The power of testimony is to give voice to the faith that
lets people run on to see what the end's gonna be.
Stories like these, told in the context of oppression,
are what the theologian Leonardo Boff calls
"testimonies charged with hope."
                              —Thomas Hoyt Jr., "Testimony"

Never Underestimate the Power of a Story
                              —Cynthia Langston Kirk, artist

Invitations

Invitations are sometimes life changing. Someone you meet at a party becomes a lifelong companion. A parent says, "Let's go outside," and on your first night in a remote area the two of you look up to see stars as you've never seen them before; and your whole perspective about the universe and your place in it changes. You go to the worship service as a polite gesture to your friend's request, but amid a jubilant congregation inspired by the music and preaching, an ecstatic feeling overtakes you and continues to open your heart to the More. The notice of the protest meeting posted on the community bulletin board causes you to attend the meeting out of curiosity; that is the beginning of your decades-long activism for environmental justice. Invitations are sometimes life changing.

This chapter illustrates how invitations take us to experiences of beloved community and personal transformation. Invitations indicate efforts to establish or sustain relationships. We are invited to a place or event where we are welcomed. Arriving, we often discover our hearts are exposed to deeper meanings of hospitality, compassion, and purpose than we anticipated. *We are enlivened to realities and relationships that enliven us to latent yearnings of our hearts.* We leave such places, but the experiences of these places and relationships continue with us. An increased sense of hope's presence continues with us. Hope embraces us through invitations.

Our lives are inundated with invitations. Invitations from our jobs, our faith communities, the array of nonprofit organizations we support, friends, people we've just met, neighborhood organizations, businesses promising to improve our lives. We cannot accept all of them. We should not. Trying to be everywhere diminishes genuine involvement anywhere. What we can do is keep our hearts open to the work that hope does through invitations. *For hope is relentless in extending invitations to be enlivened to life and experiences of beloved community.*

In addition to our personal experiences, this chapter stresses that understanding the work of hope entails meeting hope's witnesses and their stories. Our life journey is with companions, living and dead, who bear testimony to hope in their lives. Their testimonies mentor and embolden us. Yet, despite our desire and fundamental need for hope, we also resist it. It's important to know why we turn our backs on hope. If we can acknowledge the reasons, perhaps we will guard against succumbing to them. Overcoming resistance to hope and accepting the invitation to journey with hope involve choices. We have agency. The chapter concludes by inviting readers to prepare for this journey through the spiritual practices that await our taking them to heart.

Hope Is Here! is itself an invitation. The invitation to perceive hope anew is an invitation to become a people for justice and beloved community, an invitation to sing a new song, an invitation to be a practitioner of the practices, and an invitation to quest with questions. *Hope is here in invitations!*

⚜ ⚜ ⚜ ⚜ ⚜ ⚜ ⚜

The Rev. Brian Combs, my former student, invited me to see the ministry he had launched in Asheville, North Carolina. He spoke of the courses I taught on Howard Thurman's spirituality and on urban ministry, and his being introduced to liberation theology, as inspiring his subsequent involvement in Atlanta with homeless men and women, as well as his chaplaincy internship in a public hospital with patients whose medical problems were associated with extreme poverty. What he started in Asheville as the Haywood Street Congregation was an outgrowth of those Atlanta experiences.

Ministries to persons who are homeless were not new to me. I had experienced many wonderful programs of commitment and care to persons whose lives were lived on unwelcoming streets. So even though I was familiar with such ministries, I was unprepared for hope's work at Haywood Street Congregation.

Brian met me in the fellowship and administrative areas of the church. After a long embrace and expressions of delight in being together, he began to introduce me to Haywood's ministries. My first surprise came when he pointed to a room and said, "This is where we provide acupuncture to those who like the relief from pain it provides." This therapeutic offering went beyond the typical meal and clothing services given by other programs I knew. Also, instead of clothing piled on a table, Haywood's clothing was organized on racks like those you see in a department store; after looking over the selections, persons could take whatever met their physical and aesthetic needs. At a desk in the corner was a social worker who helped homeless persons to secure their disability and Social Security payments. Hanging on a wall were poetry and drawings that displayed the creativity within their community. The women and men were celebrated for their profound poetic expressions and artistic skills to image feelings.

Outside, members of the community tended a flower and organic vegetable garden that provided beauty, nutritious food, and growth of relationships. Brian told me about Haywood's new respite facility that provided those discharged from a hospital the opportunity to be housed in a safe environment that provided comfort, meals, and medical attention. This would enable persons to have a full recovery rather than returning to the streets and its dangers while physically fragile. A church service would follow the noon meal—a service in which attendance was voluntary and liturgical participation involved homeless persons.

Haywood, inside and outside, was crowded with persons who had obviously come from living on the streets to this place and time of new community. Obvious by dress. Obvious by aromas. Obvious by mental-illness behaviors. Obvious by disheveled appearance. And "new community" by the spirit of respect, care, and cooperation evidenced in relationships.

Uplifted by all this, my spirit continued to be elevated as I sat for one of the four Welcome Table lunch times. Sitting at a table for eight, with china plates, silverware, cloth napkins, and flowers, we introduced ourselves as we waited for the communal blessing. Two persons were volunteers from local churches; the other five were homeless. Haywood prohibits volunteers from serving food on their first visit. Being active in serving food can too easily become a way to avoid being in extended conversation with a homeless guest. So, volunteer activity began with cultivating heart-to-heart relationships, rather than service roles that limited conversation. Too often, feeding the hungry is done as filling an empty stomach rather than *relating with and providing food to a person who has an empty stomach.*

After the blessing, the food was brought to us in family-sized bowls and platters. One dish after another described as "homemade" was placed on our table. When a dish was fully consumed, a server would ask if we wanted more. Whether food or drink, no limit was placed on what we wanted from the many courses of the meal. Haywood's use of the word "abundance" accurately describes the experience. Abundance of welcome. Abundance of food and drink. Abundance of opportunity to converse and cultivate relationships. Abundance of care.

Around the world, being seen in table fellowship with another has been interpreted as a sign of intimacy. Jesus' morality and authority were challenged because he ate with persons accused of being betrayers and sinners. South Africa's system of apartheid required Whites and "non-Whites" to eat in separate restaurants and cafés. Segregation in the United States had both legal and local-customs enforcement against Black people and White people eating together in restaurants—and local customs could rally White-community outrage even when Black and White people ate together in their homes. Table fellowship has been understood as more than consuming food. The food that nourishes bodies also brings people together to nourish relationships. Table fellowship as a sign of intimacy is also a sign affirming the commitment to deepen relationships. Here we were at Haywood being that sign. As I tried to corral the feelings whirling in me from my experiences at Haywood, my effort suddenly released a clear and sacred declaration: "I'm experiencing beloved community!"

⚜ ⚜ ⚜ ⚜ ⚜ ⚜ ⚜

A former student invited me to go with him to a church where its worship services had made a profound impact on him. Since I had heard other students express similar feelings about the church, I was eager to accept the invitation. As we approached the Episcopal Church of the Holy Comforter, we passed many persons whose appearance did not match a stereotypical image of Sunday morning congregants. These persons' clothing looked as if they were living on the street. Most had facial expressions and physical behaviors that indicated their living with mental illness. Aromas associated with homeless living hung in the air, indicating that opportunities to shower were scarce. This lively gathering on the grounds of the church characterized the gathering I would soon experience in worship.

Most persons attending this racially diverse church were from neighborhood group homes for the mentally disabled; a significant number were homeless persons, and the rest were working and middle-class. Sitting in a pew, I was aware that this was a totally new worship environment for me. The aromas I smelled outside were also inside. Some persons moved aimlessly around the sanctuary. Several persons continued to talk either to the persons next to them or to no one in particular. Their volume ranged from conversational to loud outbursts. This continued throughout the service. Some overly active persons were accompanied by a church member who would encourage less movement or softer speaking.

In the church where I grew up, and in all the churches I had attended, any one incident of what I was seeing would have been unacceptable. Ushers were expected to intervene and escort out anyone who would/could not honor the church's decorum. However, as I looked around Holy Comforter's sanctuary, no one was in a panic.

Before long, the choir, the priest, and the other liturgy participants were in the back of the nave for the processional. As the processional music began, they advanced to the chancel with incense and singing. From that point on, the elements of worship were ones I had experienced in Episcopal and other churches. And, from that point on, the worship experience was like no other I had ever known. The behaviors of persons speaking loudly, and others deciding to walk out/in/around the sanctuary during worship, were distracting. Feelings of discomfort emerged. Would I have to contend with someone's outburst near me? Is this disruptive for the priest, the choir, the congregants? Will all this disturbance eventually settle down into a familiar decorum for worship?

As the service continued, another strong emotion overtook me. I couldn't name it, but I discovered that my body language had changed. I was relaxed. Rather than anxiously anticipating the next unsettling behavior, I was settling into worship. Songs, prayers, sermon, announcements, and greeting one another were being experienced as sacred ritual acts within a holy environment. I felt transported to a sacred place and time of community that I had always heard about and even spoken about. However, this was not what I had envisioned. *It was more than I had envisioned.*

In almost every worship service of my church life, the words "the doors of the church are open; let whosoever will, come" were declared with conviction and anticipation. Almost always, the "whosoever will" looked like those who were already members of the church. Here I was seeing a gathering made possible by "the doors of the church" having been opened by a congregation with welcoming hearts for all—including those with disruptive behaviors. I then knew that I was having one of the most profound religious experiences of my life. Holy Comforter embodied, with intentionality and grace, the teachings about Christian hospitality that I had heard throughout my life. Truly, *the word* dwelt among us and had become *worship*, and the worship had become word incarnate. It led me to name the emotion that overtook me: "I am experiencing a sacred revelation of hospitality." Hope was here, enlivening me to beloved community.

❖ ❖ ❖ ❖ ❖ ❖ ❖

My friend Don tells a story from his chaplaincy at a college. After his sermon at a worship service, a former student greeted him and during their conversation said: "One day you said something to me that changed my life." Don continued their conversation, asking about the former student's life since graduation. As the former student gave details of transitions that led to his excitement about current plans, Don's mind searched through memories of times with the young man—times that might remind him of the life-changing wisdom he had imparted. He did not want the former student to think that he had forgotten such a consequential conversation. After his failed effort to remember, Don asked, "What did I say that changed your life?" The young man answered, "You said, 'Let's go get a hamburger.'"

Don was stunned at this reply and did not understand why that invitation would be life-changing. So he asked, "Why did that change your life?" The young man said, "When I was a student here, I was obnoxious in relationships with others. I took an oppositional view to whatever someone said. Classmates responded to me by shutting off relationships. No one wanted to continue being with me after fierce contentious arguments. As isolating and detrimental as my behavior was, I relished shaping my identity in being antagonistic. However, after being in an antagonistic conversation with you, you said, 'Let's go get a hamburger.' It was the first time that anyone had offered to sustain the relationship with me after my hostile replies.

"We went to a restaurant and ate and talked. Your invitation to sustain the relationship triggered something in me. It started me on a path to understand the bitterness that was controlling my behavior. I came to realize that I had unresolved issues in the relationship with my father. Being at odds with my father transferred to being at odds with everyone. As I addressed these issues with my father, I became more engaged with people. I abandoned the need to be offensive. My current pursuit to become a minister started from your invitation that we go get a hamburger."

The Cloud of Witnesses and Their Stories

The work of hope has witnesses—some who live among us, and most who died long ago. They are authorities about its power to inspire us to "sing a new song." Their testimonies reveal and encourage. Listening and observing closely, we learn not only what hope has done for them, but also how hope may be working within us and others. Our becoming a people for justice and beloved community relies on our entering their stories and being in fellowship with them. *Hope invites us to be with the witnesses so that they enter our story.*

Christians are urged to engage their religious ancestors who guide through wisdom and example. The New Testament Letter to the Hebrews begins its roll call of exemplary individuals of faith with the first family. After speaking of Abel's offering that pleased God, the Scripture says: "He died, but through his faith he still speaks" (Heb. 11:4). The proceeding roll call lists individuals, the people of Israel, and prophets, and indicates there are even more for whom there is insufficient time to recount their stories. Chapter 12 begins, "Therefore, since we are surrounded by so great a cloud of witnesses, let us also lay aside every weight and the sin that clings so closely, and let us run with perseverance the race that is set before us." The writer then identifies Jesus as the "pioneer and perfecter of our faith," to whom we can look in the struggle to live faithfully (Heb. 12:1–2).

Even though Christians focus on Jesus as the supreme example of faithfulness, the roll call does not end with Jesus. The Orthodox and Roman Catholic churches have procedures for naming saints who are revered for their instructive lives. The names of martyrs, prophets, teachers, ascetics, activists for social change, and persons known for piety are remembered in practically all denominations. Remembering those from sacred texts, history, and even the present age is vital to the formation and sustenance we need for the faith journey. Our faith journey may go into uncharted territory, but we always have precedents of commitment and courage available in the cloud of witnesses.

The witnesses are not perfect people. In the selected Hebrews passage, we easily identify several on the roll with moral lapses: Abraham putting Sarah (his wife) at risk in his declaration that she was actually his sister, in the calculation that King Abimelech would not feel compelled to kill him in order to have Sarah for his own; Jacob's deceptions against his brother Esau; Moses killing the Egyptian; David conniving to have Bathsheba's husband killed; Rahab's life as a prostitute. So it is with our cloud of witnesses. From biblical times to the present, often those witnesses who manifest faith have vices.

A few of our witnesses may have lived almost all their days in faithful devotion to God. Others lived lives that were, at best, ordinary, if not hostile to their faith and the faithful; but at some point, when challenged to fulfill the demands of their faith, they responded in an extraordinary way. There are persons whose lives, until their dying moment, had vices galore; but they also had times of advocating for and saving lives in their communities. *Perfection is not the criterion for being in the cloud of witnesses.* The willingness to meet the ongoing and pivotal challenges of faith is what characterizes the witnesses. Though most died long ago, like Abel, through faith they still speak. The witnesses for faith are also witnesses for love and hope. They are trustworthy sources for understanding the work of hope.

⚜ ⚜ ⚜ ⚜ ⚜ ⚜ ⚜ ⚜

The cloud of witnesses is a cloud of stories. Our life journey is impoverished without an active engagement with their stories. Being familiar with the imagination and wisdom of the stories is crucial to our daily negotiation of reality. Their stories offer needed lessons that equip us to prepare, cope with adversity, and be alive to life. In the stories of these witnesses, we *experience* the work of hope for the journey.

We are a story people. Stories awaken our senses to feel love, hate, epiphany, confusion, jealousy, bonding—the full range of human emotions. We identify with characters and dramas so intensely that our emotions are stirred as we hear and see their ordeals. A story we are reading or watching may take place thousands of miles and several centuries away, but we find ourselves laughing, crying, stressed, desiring good outcomes, and wanting revenge as we are enthralled by the story unfolding before us. We struggle with characters as they face competing loyalties, inner demons, and social expectations that make the emerging lesson more real to us than a philosophical idea stripped of flesh and context. *Stories incarnate meaning.*

Jesus' use of parables is an example of his reliance on story as a medium for meaning. He portrays characters in situations where family members are in conflict, rulers make frightening pronouncements, innocent persons face assault and neglect, and wise decision-makers befuddle. The parable hooks us—enough to keep us trying to understand its meaning as we live its meaning. Even with Jesus himself, his teaching is interpreted through the story of his life. As inspiring as his words are about caring for the oppressed, knowing that he was in intimate fellowship and healing relationships with social outcasts and the diseased intensifies the meaning and power of his message of care.

Hope Is Here! emerges from stories that reveal the work of hope. Stories from my life and the lives of persons I've known who have shaped me as a witness to hope. Stories in which life is lived with vitality, despite ordeals with chronic illness, trauma, grief, and oppression. Stories of joy from lives aligned with the work of hope.

Over fifty years ago, my desire to attain a more comprehensive understanding of the power of hope led me to collect stories from newspapers and magazines about injustice, pain and suffering inflicted through neglect and hate, people overcoming adversity, persons being reborn into living life anew, and individuals committed to caring for their community. The collection has now become many file boxes of articles to which I return again and again and again to hear from the people of these stories—people who are now in my cloud of witnesses. In addition to the articles, my reading has delved into books on slavery, abolition, the civil rights struggle, colonization, consequences of war, peace movements, trauma and resilience, incarceration, disabilities, depression, chemical addiction, strategies for reducing poverty, engaging conflict creatively, dynamics of intentional communities, and spirituality. Stories from all these realities have informed me on hope's work. Throughout this book you are invited to meet some of the witnesses from these stories and to receive their testimonies about hope.

You are also invited into the stories of persons I interviewed for *Hope Is Here!* Their lives bear witness to perceiving hope in daunting personal and social realities. You will be introduced to personal and social realities of anguish and horror. I have also been introduced to witnesses in these circumstances whose lives testify to knowing free-dom, hope, and shalom.

⚜ ⚜ ⚜ ⚜ ⚜ ⚜ ⚜

Most often, discussions about hope relate to suffering and crisis—the desperation from being in "desolate pit" and "miry bog" (Ps. 40) real-ities. However, the need for hope is not limited to desperate times. Crisis amplifies the need, but hope is essential to living the ordinary days. A drowning man desperately gasping for breath, needed the air just as much when he lived his days in routine. His lungs deprived of air intensify his desperation, but his need to breathe was no less nec-essary when times were tranquil. Likewise, hope sustains, even when we are unaware of our dependence on it. *Hope is essential regardless of circumstances.*

Our challenge is to be alive to life on both the days of trauma and the days of great ease. The need for hope is as constant as the need for love. Living as a person of hope and love in serene times can be foundational to being a person of hope and love in desperate times. Consequently, the insights of this book are not relegated to our deal-ing with crisis.

Yes, the cloud of witnesses is a source that reminds, instructs, and inspires. In addition, the witnesses are looking to us to fulfill dimen-sions of faith they were unable to accomplish. After calling the roll of witnesses and their deeds, the writer of Hebrews says, "Yet all these, though they were commended for their faith, did not receive what was promised, since God had provided something better so that they would not, apart from us [we who now live], be made perfect" (Heb. 11:39–40). We look to the witnesses as icons in our resourceful past, and the witnesses look to us as promise bearers for a fulfilled future. They long to see us give fuller expression to the work of hope. They encourage and urge us.

Only God knows whether or when our lives reflect their antici-pated fulfillment. Such knowledge is beyond us. We can aspire, how-ever, to so fervently embrace life that when future generations look to the cloud of witnesses, they see us and are grateful for our life stories. *Hope is here in the witnesses and their/our stories!*

The Hope We Resist

With all the books, seminars, slogans, and songs about hope, and the nearly unanimous agreement that hope is vital to our lives, it is ironic that hope is often resisted. The reasons for this resistance are multiple, but there is a common feeling behind the reasons: *hope is more threatening than its alternatives.*

We often do not examine and try to change the present because such a process becomes a judgment on the many pivotal decisions we have made in the past. Choices made about friends, careers, health habits, moments of conflict with family members, participation in a social cause—all these and more can lead to painful scrutiny of our lives. This process of self-examination may be so painful that we refuse to do it. It may seem prudent to continue being and doing what occupies us, rather than to take inventory of our lives. As unfulfilling as the present may be, it at least provides the comfort of familiarity. Disturbing challenges and unwanted surprises are held to a minimum. Life seems more predictable, and that predictability feels reassuring. Rather than becoming more alive to life, we choose resignation. We resist hope's mandate for change, and we become willing subjects to *the tyranny of the familiar.*

Abraham (the patriarch of Judaism, Christianity, and Islam) exemplifies faithfulness in his willingness to act on God's call to newness. At age seventy-five he hears God say, "Go from your country and your kindred and your father's house to the land that I will show you. I will make of you a great nation, and I will bless you and make your name great, so that you will be a blessing" (Gen. 12:1–2). Unimagined possibilities begin when life is not determined by the tyranny of the familiar.

Hope's transformation of lives can be unsettling, disorienting, and frightening. Leaving the familiar is difficult enough. In addition, hope often takes us into precarious realities. Our lives are subjected to one uncertainty after another. The pressure gets to us, and we come to reject the belief that hope is for *us.* The biblical account of the Israelites' exodus from Egyptian bondage is full of complaint, regret, and even cynicism. Faced with danger and hardship, the people repeatedly turn their anger on Moses:

"Was it because there were no graves in Egypt that you have taken us away to die in the wilderness? What have you done to us, bringing us out of Egypt? Is this not the very thing we told you in Egypt, 'Let us alone so that we can serve the Egyptians'? For it would have been better for us to serve the Egyptians than to die in the wilderness." (Exod. 14:11–12)

The resistance to hope can be so strong that we prefer the tyranny of familiar slavery to freedom.

⚜ ⚜ ⚜ ⚜ ⚜ ⚜ ⚜

Fear of disappointment is another reason that persons resist hope. This fear blocks individuals from pursuing their dreams. As distressing and depressing as one's current situation is, embracing what appears to be a futile possibility for hope seems worse. This is especially true for persons who believe their lives are confined to environments that offer few if any options for hope.

Many years ago, I was a volunteer counselor at a Christian retreat center in Colorado that sought to influence the lives of African American youth who lived in inner-city neighborhoods of poverty and violence. Most of the youth were members of a Chicago gang. These teenagers had not only seen violence and death; some were perpetrators of neighborhood terror.

In the effort to uproot the teenagers' sense of surviving by dominance, the retreat involved them in mountain climbing, which demonstrated survival by cooperation. To counter the gang's ethic that expressing love, dreams, and fears was a sign of weakness, the retreat facilitated gatherings where the teenagers spoke and heard one another's range of emotions. New experiences of horseback riding, nonviolent sports, personal interaction with a counselor, and discovering the wilderness enabled them to experience a safe environment of nurture and adventure. The message in daily worship was of God's love and power for each of them.

Over the first five days, the whole character of the camp changed from reticence to a serious and playful engagement with relationships and questions of meaning. Belittling comments toward others diminished. Laughter was more pervasive. They confessed that the experience of not being on constant alert to attacks was strange and enjoyable. Some youth allowed themselves to cry as they spoke of a new sense of direction for their lives. They openly expressed concern for each other.

Two nights before the close of the retreat, the atmosphere of the group sessions changed from embracing new possibilities for their lives to a brooding resentment. When asked to explain the change in mood, several youths exclaimed that they had come to realize that the last five days had been a farce. As they prepared to reenter their neighborhoods, they felt that their willingness to try new ways of expressing their emotions, building relationships on love, and renouncing violence would get them harassed, beaten, and killed when they returned. They blamed the retreat staff for creating a fantasy experience that had no relevance to the places where they lived and struggled to survive. They were angry. They implied that exposing them to a vision beyond their attainment was at least naive and perhaps even cruel.

A few of the teenagers were willing to suspend judgment on the meaning of the past week until they tried these new perspectives in their Chicago surroundings. But a sizable number of the youth needed to shed the images of hope that were so meaningful and convincing to them just the day before. As they envisioned being back in inner-city Chicago, the hope discovered in the Colorado wilderness did not seem to go with them. *They feared being betrayed by hope.* They resisted hope when it seemed incapacitated by the destructive forces that defined their lives.

⚜ ⚜ ⚜ ⚜ ⚜

Our willingness to live under the tyranny of the familiar and our succumbing to the fear of disappointment are often the result of distrust of others, uncertainty about God, and a low estimate of our capacities. But behind these reasons looms a larger factor that stiffens resistance to hope: *fear of suffering.*

Fear of suffering is understandable. Avoiding and fleeing situations of suffering are instinctual and two of the most fundamental lessons taught by families. No one wants to be the victim of physical abuse or social ostracism. So our disposition against suffering, and against circumstances that might result in suffering, is natural and normal. But governing our lives by avoiding and fleeing suffering is to abandon hope—the hope that can be found in suffering and the suffering that results from living as a person of hope.

Suffering often results from decisions to move more fully into life. If I explore opportunities to form relationships with persons who are poor, I risk having my priorities and lifestyle challenged beyond defense. If I register my complaint against unethical practices at work, I risk loss of promotion or even of my job. If I take an unpopular stand on social issues, I risk alienation from friends and family. If I join demonstrations against the government's policies and practices, I risk being imprisoned and thought of as unpatriotic. We never know how far into suffering our decisions for life will take us. This uncertainty easily causes us to resist the work of hope that would take us to people, places, and issues where suffering awaits us. To say yes to hope entails risk.

This understanding of suffering is neither promoting a martyr complex nor understating the severe damage that results from suffering. Being a people for justice and beloved community involves the commitment to eliminate the suffering of others. We should do everything possible to end discrimination, abusive relationships, sexual exploitation, reckless driving, and deadly international policies. There is mass suffering for which explanation itself seems vile; only silence and grief respect the devastated reality.

In addition to the suffering that we should remedy and the suffering that we can only grieve, there is suffering we should avoid. Many experiences of suffering result from bad decision-making. Substance abuse, unhealthy eating habits, and the lack of social safety nets for people trapped in poverty are all forms of suffering to be avoided. We are enlivened to life when we eliminate and avoid suffering that torments. Still, being alive to life at times also requires us to embrace our suffering as the cost of being a sensitive and whole person.

In the work of hope, several insights emerge about suffering. First, *suffering is inevitable.* We do not live the full span of years without encountering suffering. We do not have to go looking for it; suffering will find us. The question is not, Will I suffer? Suffering is a given. The question is, Will I respond creatively to suffering? This eliminates the expenditure of resources and energy to secure oneself against all suffering. Such security does not exist. Efforts to keep all suffering at bay occur from an illusory image of life and our powers. Knowing this should lead us to employ our minds, bodies, and spirits to discern when and how suffering should be resisted, and when and how suffering should be chosen.

Second, *suffering can be revelatory* for discovering truth and responding faithfully to truth. Knowledge and wisdom result from engaging life fully. Life lived amid comfort and life lived in the midst of suffering disclose different perspectives about the human project. Novelist Léon Bloy understood this when he wrote, "In his poor heart man has places which do not yet exist and suffering enters in order to bring them to life." Something in us comes to life because of our experience with suffering. We must be careful that what emerges does not devour us, but instead tutors us in ways that *lessen* our estrangement from life and *lessons* our capabilities for life.

This revelatory and enlivening function of suffering is described in Judith Herman's *Trauma and Recovery: The Aftermath of Violence—from Domestic Abuse to Political Terror*. Herman writes about the work of therapists with survivors of atrocities. She discusses how counseling with these survivors takes an emotional toll on the therapists. The narratives of atrocities unsettle the therapists, who then struggle not only with issues of professional competence, but also with feeling overwhelmed by the horrors their clients experienced. However, Herman concludes:

> The reward of engagement is the sense of an enriched life. Therapists who work with survivors report appreciating life more fully, taking life more seriously, having a greater scope of understanding of others and themselves, forming new friendships and deeper intimate relationships, and feeling inspired by the daily examples of their patients' courage, determination, and hope.[1]

My colleague, Nancy Eiesland, wrote about her lifelong experience with severe pain. After contracting a drug-resistant staph infection, she was subjected to medical procedures that increased her disability, pain, and dependency on pain medication. She could not reverse the disability. But she decided that the pain medication kept her from functioning fully. She then *chose* to stop taking the pain medication and to return to work. She wrote:

> Finally, I return with pain, but for the first time in at least five years I do not come back on pain killers, mood elevators, or their pharmacological means to dull the ache. I say these things neither to inspire, invite your sympathy or disapproval, nor to chisel into your life in any way. I offer here my experience of pain to remind us that for most of us pain will be an ordinary partner in an ordinary life. The social fiction that long-term pain ought to be treated with more and better drugs is an attractive one.
>
> But even when it is severe and unremitting, I am persuaded that pain is a better friend than is the pain killer. As my life began to reveal, one never can be sure what else with you dies when you try to kill the pain.[2]

The testimony of Herman and Eiesland is consistent with that of saints throughout the ages and of the wisest among us. At times, intentionally moving deeper into suffering becomes a way to a fuller life. What an irony! Hope seeks to save us from the suffering of being alienated from life, so hope takes us into the suffering of life. We come to realize that suffering is not the ultimate concern of hope. Our wholeness (salvation) is. Suffering is not the purpose but is the vehicle to an experience of freedom and wholeness. The apostle Paul writes, "We also boast in our sufferings, knowing that suffering produces endurance, and endurance produces character, and character produces hope, and hope does not disappoint us" (Rom. 5:3–5 RSV). Our embrace of suffering can end our estrangement from embracing life fully. *Our embrace of suffering can be a witness to the work of hope.*

In his book *Disciplines of the Spirit*, Howard Thurman speaks of suffering, not just as something that happens to us, but as a choice of faithfulness. This is no appeal to masochism. Neither is it acceptance of injustices perpetrated against humanity. When suffering can be resisted and reduced, we should participate in such healing activity. However, opportunities to love and work for justice often require us to take a path on which the buzzards are circling and suffering, if not death, is assured.

If we fail to follow God's call because we are intimidated by suffering, then our fear of suffering has more power over us than our devotion to God. The threat and fear of suffering manipulate our commitment. Thurman offers a way to be liberated by suffering instead of enslaved. He asserts that suffering is not only the encounter with pain, but also a discipline—that is, something one does by choice.[3] When we embrace suffering as a choice, we can be on the journey to which God calls us, regardless of the suffering we anticipate. Then we engage life with a freedom and compassion that suffering does not control.

Resigning our lives to the tyranny of the familiar, fear of disappointment, and fear of suffering is to resist the work of hope. Any one or a combination of these factors can convince us that hope is not always for us. This conclusion is understandable, but deadly. Ironically, it results in our lives being separated from the peace (wholeness) that God intended for us—a peace that surpasses all understanding. To resist hope is to resist the freedom necessary to be on the journey toward a more fulfilling life.

Choosing Life, Choosing Hope, Choosing Preparation

We are created with a heart for hope. Each of us has a deep longing to embrace fully the adventure of living. Yet, despite having a heart for hope, we often resist the very hope that endeavors to enliven us to life. What must we do to be liberated from choosing bondage when hope offers freedom?

Several years ago, while jogging in my neighborhood, I came upon a woman, her daughter who looked about seven years old, and their dog. The little girl saw me approaching, her eyes widened, and with an outburst of energy she ran alongside me. To keep up, she had to take two quick steps to my one. Despite this extra effort, she was able to talk while running.

"Do you want to pat my dog?" she asked.

Being in a hurry to achieve a good running time, I kept my pace and simply replied, "No, thank you."

She continued, "I like my dog. Do you have a dog?"

"No, not now, but I used to," I answered.

I could tell that my pace was tiring for her, but she sustained the conversation by saying, "You run really fast. Do you run races?"

I answered, "No, not now, but I used to."

Now exhausted, she stopped as I continued. I turned to see her spread her arms far apart and yell: "Sounds to me like you *used to* live a big life!"

When I heard this last response, I laughed. In part I laughed because of her quick and comprehensive conclusion from this short exchange. In the naiveté of a child's world, having a dog and running races were indicators of living a "big life."

I also laughed because of the wisdom spoken beyond the specific reference to my life. Adults can so easily go from big dreams and fulfilling activities to life patterns devoid of an enlivening embrace of life. When asked about the initiatives taken for joy and meaning in our lives, we too often refer to past behaviors that are not continued in the present. Taking time to focus on life and its significance, playfulness in physical recreation, time with friends, exploring places and ideas, envisioning and working on behalf of a more just and caring world— all these and more are initiatives associated with early phases of life. Our response to questions about sustaining such experiences as adults is often, "No, not now, but I used to." Our dedication to living a "big life" is more memory than current living. Of course, we have our justifications for this: growing older means assuming responsibilities that did not consume the time and energy of our youth, or the demands and "wisdom" of adulthood extinguish the idealism of youth.

The determination to live a big life too frequently becomes a dream deferred. However, we are not fated to live small. Choosing to embrace hope is our agency. The five spiritual practices in the coming chapters are means for empowering our embrace. Beyond helping us to overcome resistance to hope, the practices fuel our "response ability" to live a big life.

❧❧❧❧❧❧❧

Having "response ability," however, does not result in a rush to enact the practices in our lives. Singing a new song may involve altering behaviors that now consume our time and energy. If only we could conclude that current behaviors were ruinous, then we might contest how we are living. But irresponsible behavior is not usually the situation. Most often our routines are devoted to family obligations, careers, recreation, and sustaining social relationships established over the years. These routines can be satisfying, as they exhaust all our waking hours. We admire the vision of beloved community, even as we fail to see how more of ourselves can be available to it. Consequently, we are left with the conclusion that although the work of hope appeals to us, it also appears to be beyond our capability.

Becoming new is not about forsaking current routines—although it could be. Becoming new is not about devoting ourselves to causes other than what we now do—although it could be. Each person's transformation into becoming new will have its distinctive opportunities and challenges. No one-size-fits-all blueprint exists. The newness is about becoming more alive to life and the vision of community that God dreams for us. Are our current routines and causes sufficient vessels for the work of hope in our lives? Jesus warned about the failure from entrusting old containers with the vitality of new content: "No one puts new wine into old wineskins; otherwise, the new wine will burst the skins and will spill out, and the skins will be ruined. But new wine must be put into fresh wineskins" (Luke 5:37–38). It's important to examine and assess the capacities of our wineskins to carry what is vital for us and beloved community.

The spiritual practices are integral to the work of hope. They help us discern whether our routines, relationships, and commitment are sufficient for enlivening our true selves and beloved community. As we seek to be fully alive, the practices prepare us in the lifelong journey with hope. Seeking is the spiritual way for taking the adventure of life seriously, and preparation takes seeking seriously. Would you really want to seek (to be journey bound) without preparation? Preparation changes the readiness of the person bound for a journey, it changes the experience of a journey, and it empowers journeys that change the world.

Many persons who joined the civil rights movement in the 1950s and 1960s were unprepared to participate in the movement's non-violent tactics. These individuals came into the movement preconditioned to fight or flee when assaulted. The movement made new demands upon them to absorb blows from police batons and angry mobs. Before they could join a sit-in protest or march, they were trained to respond in nonviolent ways to anticipated abuse. This preparation so transformed many of the demonstrators that they experienced freedom from oppression long before any of the civil rights laws were enacted. The preparation itself gave persons a new sense of their capacities to overcome fear and systemic violence. Even contemplating their own deaths in a protest did not foreclose their hopefulness. Joining the movement and being trained in nonviolent activism had liberated them from acquiescence or ineffective responses to their oppression. Preparation made an immediate difference with the activists—a difference that resonated with the final goals of the movement.

Preparation is more than the effort to get ready for a journey. Preparation is integral to every step of a journey. Thinking of preparation as only prelude to a journey establishes a false separation between preparation and the journey itself. This separation tends to cast preparation as the onerous tasks that must be accomplished *before* the adventure of journey begins. Such a distinction diminishes the profound significance of the preparation experience. Preparation itself transforms. Preparation is not just a prelude to the transformation that occurs on the journey; *transformation (the work of hope) begins and is sustained with preparation.*

All five spiritual practices prepare us to be enlivened by hope. They mentor and empower our hopefulness. The practices take us on a journey into the past, present, and future. They transport us as time travelers. As children of history, we are wise to visit the times and people who birthed the realities that birthed our current realities. As faith pilgrims and citizens in the present, we are obligated to care actively by nurturing our authentic selves and beloved community. As parents of the future, we must be attentive to coming realities born by both our neglect and our compassion.

Choosing "a big life" entails choosing hope. Choosing hope entails choosing preparation. We have the freedom to choose. Nothing could be more consequential than our deciding rightly.

Hope is here! Hope is persistent, but not coercive. We have choices. As we journey with the practices, they will make demands on our time, energy, and comfort zones. In the work of hope, the transforming power of the practices can be disturbing and painful, reassuring and joyful, as they fulfill the deepest hunger of our hearts. *Hope is here in the spiritual practices!*

A rich ruler asks Jesus, "Good Teacher, what must I do to inherit eternal life?" Jesus responds, "Sell all that you own and distribute the money to the poor, and you will have treasure in heaven; then come, follow me" (Luke 18:18–22). The ruler is sad because he chooses attachment to his riches over the requirements of "eternal life" and following Jesus. Choices, even ones that hold wondrous promise, are frequently rejected because *we resist entrusting our lives to hope*. We succumb to our insecurities and fears, and then choose against "a big life."

Hope is here *for us!* It invites us to places, relationships, and causes where we experience new awareness and opportunities for coming alive. As mentioned in this chapter's stories, it often achieves its transformative purpose by having others extend invitations to us. Hope turns us to see its stories in the cloud of witnesses who surround us. We have their testimonies as immediate inspiration and guidance for our faith journey. Some witnesses and their stories we know well. Lingering with them is crucial to honoring their presence with us. Other witnesses in our faith tradition and personal lives are unknown by us. We are wise to invite ourselves into their stories through study and pilgrimages to where they might speak to us.

As I have said, at times our major resistance to becoming hopeful is not failing to see hope's immediacy, but not trusting it to respect our aversion to disappointment and suffering. To resist hope is to resist how God endeavors to enliven us. This leads to the most fundamental question in spiritual formation: "Do I trust God with my life?" Our answer to this question characterizes if and how we give ourselves to hope and become a people for beloved community. Hope is available so that we will answer "Yes!"

Discerning among invitations received and invitations to send involves making choices that have clear and ambiguous outcomes. Prioritizing what is most relevant to living "a big life" is not easy. The spiritual practices deepen our capacities to discern and prioritize wisely. They prepare us to live faithfully and abundantly. Hope, in its enlivening work, longs for us to choose the forthcoming practices.

Questing with Questions

1. What life-changing invitations have you received? Reflect on the circumstances of one of these invitations and what made it life changing for you.
2. What invitations have you extended that have been consequential to others? Reflect on your feelings about such outcomes.
3. Reflecting on the story of the Episcopal Church of the Holy Comforter, how might experiencing "disruption" be transformative for your spiritual formation?
4. Write down the names of those in your cloud of witnesses. What in their examples informs who you are? What inspires you? What troubles you? What lessons do they teach you about hope? Note their race, gender, ethnicity, period of history, vocation. How are they similar and different? Among them, to what persons do you listen most, and why? Who else do you need in your cloud of witnesses?
5. Do you identify with any of the stated reasons in this chapter for resisting hope? If so, reflect on times when you've resisted and on why you resisted. What have you done, or what are you doing, to overcome your resistance to hope?
6. What are your questions from reading this chapter?

Chapter Three

Contemplative Praying

The outer work can never be small if the inner work is great, neither can the outer be great or good if the inner is little or nothing.
—Meister Eckhart, *The Book of Divine Comfort*

Here is the truth! Go where you will, to Benares or to Mathura; if you do not find your soul, the world is unreal to you.
—*Songs of Kabir*, translated by Rabindranath Tagore

The Call to Prayer

"Prayer changes things" is more than a pious cliché. Praying transforms us. As we open our hearts to God—whether from gratitude, rejoicing, grief, confusion, or anxiety—we declare that our life's journey relies upon God's love and guidance. Prayer is a means by which heart communicates with Heart. Suffocating delusions of self-sufficiency are expelled. Though the Beloved Companion is "closer to us than we are to ourselves," the very act of praying declares our desire to experience God's presence in a distinctive way. After an openhearted encounter with God, we are never the same.

Hope enlivens us through prayer. We become hopeful in experiencing intimacy with God in prayer. Even with daunting life challenges that await, the prayerful certainty of God's abiding presence assures us that we can be alive to life and for life. The privilege of speaking our hearts to God in prayer "changes things." We are changed by the ability to announce what delights us and what distresses us. God hears us!

Still, the personal and communal transformations we seek for justice and beloved community entail more than naming concerns in times of prayer. Prayer involves not only *what we say* but also *our need to listen.* Contemplative praying enables us to hear what hope is saying to us. Though contemplative praying is immediately accessible, being "at home" in it may involve trusting new experiences of listening, discernment, and engaging. This chapter invites readers to embrace contemplative praying as a spiritual practice that enlivens us to ourselves and to become a people for beloved community. Contemplative praying is a continuum of listening, discerning, and engaging. *Each of the phases is crucial to the others; and all the phases are crucial to the transformative power of contemplative praying.* Sometimes we discover that "prayer changes things (including us)" because *how we pray has changed.*

✣ ✣ ✣ ✣ ✣ ✣ ✣

Praying is so fundamental to religion that we often assume religious practitioners are certain about prayer and praying. This is not necessarily so. Uncertainty about praying befalls persons who question their readiness to speak to God. Must their life be purer before entering into prayer? Do they need a religious official to pray on their behalf? What do they do with their doubts that come from previous prayers that they believe God failed to answer? Should anger with God be expressed in prayer? Should they bargain with God in prayer? For praying to be effective, are there necessary prayer postures?

Consequently, our hunger to pray is accompanied by our hunger to be guided in praying faithfully. Jesus' disciples had this hunger to be guided in prayer, even after they had traveled with, listened to, and served with him throughout his ministry. After Jesus had finished a time of prayer, one of his disciples said, "Lord, teach us to pray, as John taught his disciples" (Luke 11:1). The disciples wanted guidance in how to be present and communicate with God so that they might be as fully alive to God as was Jesus. They had heard Jesus talk about God. They had observed Jesus in prayer. Still, they wanted more;

they wanted to be taught so that their praying was truly grounded in the same consciousness that Jesus brought to prayer and experienced in praying. This Scripture conveys that prayer, although personal, is a spiritual practice for which we sometimes seek and need guidance to deepen our praying. Offering our time and hearts to contemplative praying is such an opportunity to go deeper.

Prayer, as communication with God, is essential for taking our relationship with God seriously. Prayer is a means by which we come to know the nature and necessity of our relationship with God. Consider a personal relationship in which you are deeply in love—a relationship in which the intensity of feelings is mutually felt. Now imagine that you have means to communicate with one another—telephones, letter writing, email, travel—but no communication occurs. The failure to communicate would be a crisis for the relationship. We might ask, Are the feelings of love as deep as I thought? What is preventing us from contacting one another? How serious are we about this relationship? The failure to pray raises similar relationship-defining questions that indicate crisis in our relationship with God. *Hope is here in the call to prayer!*

The Listening Heart

Contemplative praying is a heart-opening expression of prayer. Rather than starting by speaking our confessions, concerns, desires, and gratitude, contemplative praying often begins with establishing a mood or disposition that enables us to listen deeply, a procedure called "centering." This involves being in a place where we are not distracted by phone calls, environmental noises demanding attention, interruptions from people, and our own compulsions to be busy. The intention is to be fully available to this prayerful time. Silence or meditative music, stillness, repeatedly reciting a meaningful word or phrase, a relaxed sitting posture or walking, eyes closed or focused on a single object, selecting a particular place in a room or in nature are all means to prepare and be receptive to what comes forth as we center ourselves.

A major challenge for centering is distractions that come not only from persons and responsibilities demanding our immediate attention, but also from thoughts that interrupt our becoming still and focused on being available fully to the contemplative opportunity. When I visited a meditation center, the instructor helped all of us to settle into a comfortable posture that would assist our minds to be still and center. He then said: "We are located next to a bus stop. While meditating, you will hear a bus arrive just a few feet away from us. It's normal and acceptable to hear the bus. This need not cancel your experience of meditating. The key is to not allow your mind to wander by wondering where the bus is going, or to imagine you've entered the bus and can identify scenes along its route. Resist pursuing the distraction!" Since then, the instructor's guidance has returned me to contemplative opportunities, despite impulses to pursue internal and external distractions.

Centering ushers one into a contemplative mood. A new sense of awareness may first characterize the prayer time—maybe an awareness that cannot be translated into speech. Perhaps feelings, thoughts, insights, and even words emerge from the contemplation. All this comes from an acute attentiveness to being with God. These contemplative praying procedures for readiness are our way of announcing, "I am here, and I am listening."

Listening is fundamental to the faith journey. Moses contends with the Israelites' refusal to *listen* to his liberating message that God will deliver them from bondage to freedom (Exod. 6:9). The prophets continually implore God's people to *listen* to God's messages of justice and compassion. Jesus calls his followers to *listen* (Luke 8:8,18). At the transfiguration, God declares Jesus' identity and the imperative that his companions "listen to him!" (Luke 9:34–35). God is with us, providing instructive examples through sacred history, prophets, and witnesses. *They are sources for our being enlivened to life by hope.* The sources guide and inspire. Their transformative power, however, relies on our listening. *Contemplative praying is a spiritual practice grounded in listening as it cultivates listening.*

How well do you listen to the God who dwells with you? How do you prepare a prayer-meeting space and time where you hold at bay the frenzy of responsibilities, incessant decision-making, the assault of news, and requests for your time? How do you give yourself a space and time to hear what is felt, and to feel what is heard, when the mind becomes still, and silence amplifies what is being whispered from the depths?

Listening to God who dwells in us and listening to our authentic selves may be the same experience. This does not necessarily equate the authentic self and God. Still, *the authentic self is not only a sacred expression of God; its enlivening power expresses God.* On a personal level, we have important questions to engage: How am I listening prayerfully for who God created me to be and become? What is my authentic self affirming about my identity and capabilities? How is my sense of identity, for better or for worse, shaped by others and my responses to circumstances? What causes me to distort the sacred image that God created me to be? How am I honoring my authentic self in the moments of each day?

It is so easy to move through each day ignoring our authentic selves. Perhaps we feel swept away day after day by an avalanche of meetings, responsibilities, time-consuming interruptions, incessant messages wanting our attention and response, going somewhere, returning from somewhere. If we are asked, "*Who are you when you're not busy?*" our most immediate answers might defer to *how we feel* rather than *who we are.* Common responses are "I'm tired," "I'm bored," "I'm anxious," "I feel lost," "I feel that I'm neglecting work that needs completion." The most avoided—but most revealing—answer to the question is, "I don't know."

Hope's mission to enliven us to life involves guiding us to listen deeply to our authentic selves. Our authentic selves assure us of our worthiness and capability. We are more than our failed opportunities, major achievements, public acclaim, and worst mistakes. The ability to live creatively and more fully is possible despite circumstances of mental and physical disabilities, toxic relationships, an oppressive society, trauma, and imprisonment. All such circumstances have witnesses whose lives testify to their authentic selves consoling and empowering them to resilience.

A turning point in Martin Luther King Jr.'s life occurred during his leadership of the civil rights struggle in Montgomery, Alabama. Death threats were constant. The toll from these threats led him to a "saturation point" where he was "ready to give up." Feeling over-whelmed and depleted, he prayed. He describes what occurred next:

At that moment I experienced the presence of the Divine as I had never experienced Him before. *It seemed as though I could hear the quiet assurance of an inner voice* [italics added] saying: "Stand up for righteousness, stand up for truth; and God will be at your side forever." Almost at once my fears began to go. My uncertainty disappeared. I was ready to face anything.[1]

King's listening heart heard what was needed to continue in hope and on behalf of hope.

In his groundbreaking book *The Body Keeps the Score: Brain, Mind, and Body in the Healing of Trauma*, Bessel van der Kolk reports on Dr. Richard Schwartz's work on mindfulness (a meditation practice similar to contemplative praying) used in his family therapy practice. In addressing devastating consequences from traumatic experiences, Schwartz makes two discoveries that van der Kolk says are confirmed by neuroscience:

> Beneath the surface of the protective parts of trauma survivors there exists an undamaged essence, a Self that is confident, curious, and calm, a Self that has been sheltered from destruction by the various protectors that have emerged in their efforts to ensure survival. Once those protectors trust that it is safe to separate, the Self will spontaneously emerge, and the parts can be enlisted in the healing process.
>
> The second assumption is that, rather than being a passive observer, this mindful Self can help reorganize the inner system and communicate with the parts in ways that help those parts trust that there is someone inside who can handle things.[2]

The conclusions of the therapist and neuroscience have been the testimony of religious teachers for centuries. A phrase in the Quaker tradition for encountering "the inward teacher in action" is *"we have come down to the place that knows."*[3] Within us is a God-given resource (the authentic self) that heals and empowers us to live in the present and future with confidence and hopefulness. We are wise to listen for it.

❧❧❧❧❧❧❧

The listening heart is not only assured and guided by one's own authentic self; the heart listens for the God who dwells in others. Contemplative listening is a way to be in prayerful relationship with another. Blocking internal and external distractions, the listener is more fully available to expressed feelings and thoughts. Care is taken to not interrupt. Debating with counterarguments is suspended. Assessing another's intelligence or moral rectitude is absent. The listening heart endeavors to be enlivened to life by being centered with others. At times the centering pulls back the veil on another's carefully chosen words—words that speak feelings and create graphic images of meaning—so that we understand more clearly. Paying attention to the words is important. In addition, changes in facial expressions, hesitations, silence, and tears may point to what is behind the words and beyond words.

The power of listening overtook me on a pastoral visit to a member of my church. The visit was in response to his wife's request. He was in a rehabilitation center and had not had many visitors. She felt my visit would cheer him up. She alerted me to his difficulty in speaking because of the surgery to remove a tumor from his brain. Thinking I might spare him the frustrations from speaking, I brought a book of meditations to read to him.

Entering the room, I was completely unprepared for the image of the man I had known. The concave depression in his skull was massive. The surgery had removed a large section of his brain. I was shocked by his disfigured head. Aware that a shocked expression might be disheartening for him to see, I rallied my emotions to not alter his smiling welcome. After conveying my joy for this time to visit, I asked the customary, "How are you?" His response was a jumble of sounds given with enthusiasm, but nothing that resembled words. His wife's statement that he has "difficulty in speaking" was not even close to describing his unintelligible effort.

I continued by expressing how good it was to see him and how the church was upholding him in prayer. Smiling, he gave a lengthy response that might as well have been a forgotten ancient language. Surmising that conversation would not be the order of the day, I asked if he would like for me to read from the book of meditations. He smiled and nodded yes. I read. At the end of the reading, he uttered another lengthy response. When he had concluded, I offered to read another meditation. Again, he nodded agreement. After the reading, he answered with an enthusiastic and long retort that convinced me that he was more interested in conversation than listening to me read.

I closed the book, composed my anxious spirit, and began the conversation by saying that I would soon be moving to Atlanta. As before, his response was immediate, lengthy, and unintelligible. Yet nothing in our communicating was the same. I listened . . . really listened. I no longer focused on the absence of words. I relaxed attempts to hear familiar language. I gave myself to being fully present to these moments of togetherness. I listened.

When he paused, I said, "You're telling me that you came to St. Louis from Georgia." With the biggest smile of our visit, he nodded yes. I continued, "You came here on the train to find work." Again, the affirming headshake. "And you began doing custodial work in many different places before arriving at the company where you retired." His whole body was now involved in saying yes. Our conversation continued for another half-hour. Ending the visit, we hugged, and I left in a daze. Nothing like this had ever happened with me. I could not make sense of how it occurred. Still, I felt that I had experienced being in a miracle.

The next Sunday, I greeted his wife and told her about our conversation. She was astonished. She struggled to believe that I could understand him because she and no one else could. My report to her on the conversation matched details of his life. Oddly, even before his wife confirmed the details of my conversation with her husband, I was certain about their veracity.

I cannot explain how this occurred. My best notion is that my authentic self knew I needed to become *still* so that my listening and understanding could become *active*. This stillness was the aforementioned "mood or disposition" for contemplative prayer. The effort to "manage" a conversation was relinquished. Listening with a greater depth of myself was heart opening, and this active listening overcame reliance on discernable speech. The connection we made was the sacred experience of communion. Not only was our communication transformed by the experience, but we were also transformed.

Contemplative listening was more than a prelude to prayer or analogous to prayer. *Contemplative listening was contemplative praying.* As I listened, my heart became more available and enlivened to my church member and God's presence. This is the work of hope.

✤ ✤ ✤ ✤ ✤ ✤ ✤

Even within our customary ways of communicating, the listening heart introduces new opportunities for engaging and hearing one another. This is vital when addressing the alienation that plagues our interpersonal relationships and societal interactions. Where separation and self-segregation exist because of racial, ethnic, economic, sexual orientation, and political differences, dehumanizing stereotyping and behaviors follow. This alienation among people is not a pre-crisis situation; the alienation *is the crisis.* Increasing understanding and respect is essential to forming beloved community characterized by compassion and justice. Fundamental to understanding and respect is listening deeply to another.

We will return to listening as a means for overcoming alienation and adversity in the chapters "Crossing Identity Boundaries" and "Transforming Conflict." Right now, my emphasis is on recognizing that a contemplative mind-set in communication, one that has been formed by contemplative praying, can increase understanding another's heart. When listening deeply, I abandon being in battle mode where I'm focused on making self-defense and attack arguments. Rather than targeting weaknesses to exploit, I search for questions to clarify my/our understanding. Moreover, *I'm listening for my authentic self to guide my sense of identity and purpose in overcoming alienation.*

The listening heart plays a major role in subduing anxieties and stereotypes that stoke alienation among races and ethnicities. The "other" is *met.* Our authentic selves hear the sorrows and joys of another's authentic self. Though the experiences may be vastly different, a recognition of common significance occurs. Alienation diminishes as understanding increases.

Overcoming alienation is also disruptive. When persons are no longer reduced to caricatures, both the perceived and perceiver are changed. Uprooting bias alters the identity landscape. For example, to speak of an "undocumented immigrant" rather than "illegal alien" has implications beyond government policies. The change in language reflects a change in heart; and the heart questions how the seeds of bias and alienation were planted. What led me to have a distorted image of these immigrants (and/or refugees)? How does my new perspective influence my interactions with them? Will I be an activist on their behalf? How will I now relate to family and friends who still foster these caricatures?

Another example of listening to overcome alienation is the controversy over the phrase "Black lives matter." The organization Black Lives Matter was founded to protest the killing of Black people by law enforcement officers and vigilantes. The organization's protest tactics have received both praise and condemnation. However, the phrase has developed a life beyond its founding organization—so much that its use has come to indicate where individuals stand in acknowledging the inordinate danger and death that Black people face in society.

Persons adverse to the phrase often retort, "All lives matter." Or those who believe the phrase is an attack upon law enforcement will assert, "Blue lives matter." The reaction against speaking the phrase (especially by many White persons) is exceedingly strong. When some persons are asked, "Can you say, 'Black lives matter?'" their frequent and repeated response that "*all* lives matter" suggests they are hearing that "*only* Black lives matter." Why is this? What factors cajole persons to insert "only" into the phrase, and to then insist that it's implied, even after being told otherwise? Are they avoiding the realities of racism and how these realities have shaped their country, associations, and personal identity? Do they refuse to acknowledge that Black lives are more threatened by lethal force? Do they believe that Black lives *don't* matter?

A different set of questions about the listening heart goes beyond the phrase "Black lives matter" to the long-standing messages of pain and injustice spoken by Black people. Why are the fears and grieving from the Black community ignored? Why can't marches and shouts of protest be heard as a cry for community healing? Considering that Black outrage against abusive law enforcement and a biased judicial system has been voiced loudly for decades, why did it take the video of George Floyd's death to open and impact the listening heart of so many?

Oppression flourishes because of hardened hearts that do not listen. In a primary biblical story of God's liberating demand and action, Moses and Aaron confront Pharaoh with God's message: "Let my people go." Pharaoh refuses. Each refusal is characterized as Pharaoh's heart being "hardened" (Exod. 7–14). Repeatedly, with a hardened heart, Pharaoh "does not listen to them." In this biblical narrative, refusing to listen to God's messengers is synonymous with refusing to listen to God. We are challenged to hear God's message because we often doubt the messengers. Do they have credentials that we respect? Are they likable? How are we certain they have received a holy message?

The listening heart is open to the many ways God's liberating message is delivered. In those times when our own lives have been inattentive to praying and/or to oppressive realities, we are wise to listen to God's messengers—those who suffer injustice and those who have been openhearted in listening to God. They reveal what is required to save us from continuing to live in communities of oppression and alienation. We must be careful that our criteria for assessing their worthiness as messengers are not hardening our hearts to the message.

This last point of listening to God's messengers is illustrated in the environmental crises of climate change, pollution, deforestation, and excessive irrigation. Our hearts have been slow to listen to the cries of the earth. Although nature has screamed its wounds for decades, we "did not listen" at levels of personal responsibility, collective behaviors, and governmental action. As in the visit with my church member who could not speak words, we must give ourselves to new ways of listening to the earth's efforts to speak to us. Where we fail to hear clearly, we should prayerfully listen to those whose hearts are attuned to listening to nature's plight. They are God's messengers. *Hope is here with the messengers and our listening hearts* to enliven us to hear God's liberating call to the promised land (beloved community).

The Discerning Heart

After Jesus' baptism, he experienced God's affirming, "This is my Son, the Beloved, with whom I am well pleased" (Matt. 3:17). Still, Jesus needed to discern the path for his ministry. The Spirit led him into the wilderness. In this place removed from the usual rhythms of his life, he gave himself to fasting—a means to intensify his prayerful time with God. After many days, he was famished. In addition to his physical ordeal, he experienced the spiritual ordeal to resist temptations that defied God's authority over his life. In overcoming each temptation, Jesus recited passages from Deuteronomy that spoke directly to the challenges. Sacred Scripture was a resource for discerning his way forward. These would not be his last days of discernment. However, what he experienced on these days would be available for his discerning heart on all the days that followed.

Baptism is a Christian ritual that declares publicly a personal commitment to follow in the Way of Jesus. The ritual may require candidates for baptism to answer questions about the church's doctrines and their willingness to live according to them, their willingness to repent of sins, and their participation in the church's mission. Still, the time of baptism does not come with an answer book to the thousands of complex challenges and questions that arise in all the days that follow. The discerning heart is essential for persons to honor their baptismal vow to follow in the Way of Jesus.

Contemplative praying's emphasis on establishing a place and time that enhances the ability to focus and *listen* is novel for many. This is so unconventional (even though it's an ancient Christian way of praying) that the new behaviors of preparation and listening are often interpreted as defining contemplative praying. However, a contemplative prayer does not end in listening. Whether still in the chosen time and environment for contemplative listening or months later, while involved in rhythms of work and rest, *we continue in contemplative prayer by discerning what we have heard.* Discernment insights might arise in a covenantal group, from a surprising encounter with a friend or stranger, or reading. In the open heart's effort to derive meaning from life experiences, it never ceases praying.

Contemplative praying relies upon discernment, and discernment relies upon our deep listening to God's leading within us. This embrace of oneself for trustworthy discernment is stressed in Parker Palmer's *Let Your Life Speak.* Writing on the process of discernment for vocation, he says:

Discovering vocation does not mean scrambling toward some prize just beyond my reach but accepting the treasure of the true self I already possess. . . . It comes from a voice "in here" calling me to be the person I was born to be, to fulfill the original selfhood given me at birth by God.[4]

Without *deep* listening, discernment is likely based upon listening to our fears, ambitions, and inauthentic selves. Prayer is the opportunity for our listening and discerning hearts to choose the most faithful way forward.

Contemplative praying is a vital means for discerning among the choices for experiencing hope's power to enliven us to life. Discovering a truer answer may require more time, focus, and study. Our most difficult choices are usually not between what is blatantly bad and a clearly good option. The most complicated decisions on the faith journey involve choosing what best honors God's dream for us and beloved community. For example, not spreading gossip about a neighbor's shameful behaviors can be thoughtful and caring. Choosing to engage the neighbor with uplifting conversation and expressions of hospitality is a very different choice to discern.

The discerning heart is integral to prayer. As we gain insight while praying, we may also perceive new possibilities to surrender our lives to God's forces of love and hope. Some of these possibilities compete with one another. Am I being called to devote myself to the needs of my city or to crises in a distant land? Do I leave current obligations, or do I wait until my family is more settled? Some of the possibilities raise questions about underlying motivations. Do I really forgive her, or am I just needing to sustain the relationship to advance my social standing? Am I not going to the antiracism workshop because I'm overly committed to community projects, or am I refusing to go because I'm anxious about dealing with anticipated racial conflict? The discerning heart endeavors to listen deeply for the true self to identify options most aligned with the work of hope.

※ ※ ※ ※ ※ ※ ※

The discerning heart looks both within and externally to interpret what it prayerfully contemplates. Formed in community, our hearts look to community as a place that offers us relationships that support our quest for insight. Teachers, family members, friends, pastors, counselors, and spiritual directors are just a few of the many persons whose life experiences and professional training can provide perspectives for our inward teacher to consider. Community is also a "place that knows."

Quaker practices involve "the meeting" (those gathered for worship and church business) in discerning God's leading on communal matters. The belief that *the Divine moves within all* to bring forth a right understanding or decision is so strong that additional gatherings may be scheduled to honor the needed time for unity. Discerning correctly entails patience. Community, in this instance, is not just a place from which personal guides emerge; God moves to inspire the whole community to arrive with a discerned outcome.

Whether with personal guides, the meeting, or a clearance committee (four to six persons gathered to help an individual or couple with a pivotal life decision), deep listening is required to honor the movement of God within each person and among the community. Our authentic selves and the Holy Spirit are joined in speaking to us and for us. Quaker scholar Michael L. Birkel characterizes this listening to self and God as one process:

> As we listen to divine guidance, our true desires are clarified. Central to discernment is discovering our deepest desires, where we are truly in tune with God's desire for humankind. The deepest human desire is to be loved and accepted by God. . . . As we 'attend to that Holy Spirit which sets right bounds to our desires', we find our truest desire. Rather than renouncing power, wealth, and honour in a noble sacrifice, we simply discover that they no longer hold such interest for us. The dissatisfying substitute has yielded to the genuine substance.[5]

Discernment, like deep listening, is an expression of prayer. Alone or with others, the heart is given to being alive to life by being alive to God's presence and leading.

Each discerning heart is informed by sources. These questions are for every person: Who and what do I consider to be credible sources for my discernment? What messengers do I trust? What qualifies others (individuals or groups/committees) to be entrusted with my discerning heart? What disqualifies others? These are not just cerebral questions. Consciously or not, we arrive at major decisions after the discriminating work of determining who is worthy of our listening to them and our trust. Equally crucial is understanding who and what are dismissed as having less value in our formation. Discerning hearts benefit from identifying their trusted sources.

This significance of identifying sources for discernment is illustrated in Brian Combs's founding of Haywood Street Congregation in Asheville (see chapter 2). In my interview of Brian, I asked what enabled him to persist in launching his ministry with homeless persons. After all, his church authorities' qualms about his vision led to their insistence that he attend a new church startup "boot camp" (yes, this was the official term for it)—a camp that turned out to be unenthusiastic about his vision. The camp's attendees and instructors were focused on church planting in fast-growing suburban areas where membership growth and financial sustainability were most probable. Nothing discussed related to his desire to establish an urban ministry based on welcoming and "being church" with homeless persons. Brian reflects that in his exit interview the camp's assessment committee members were "unequivocal in saying, 'Your vision for ministry simply is untenable; it's not going to work, and we cannot endorse it.'"

The discernment of boot camp officials was disappointing, but not determinative for Brian. Remembering his urban ministry experiences in Atlanta was more compelling. He especially references conversations he had with a former pimp (someone who controls prostitution arrangements) about life on city streets. When Brian signed into a homeless shelter to have a firsthand experience of its realities, the former pimp (Brian does not recall the man giving his name) also signed in to protect Brian from foreboding areas of the shelter and dangerous interactions. At some point during the night, the man indicated he wanted Brian to "get a little rest" and then volunteered to stay awake to assure Brian's safety. This caring act impacted Brian. Because of this and other such experiences, Brian says, "The notion of mission . . . was inverted for me." He kept "bumping into God's incarnation" in those who are too often understood to be only subjects of Christian outreach. Brian began to "reimagine Jesus" in persons who did not resemble Brian or his culture. He professed that these interactions were "my deep sense of calling."

The discernment that resulted in the Haywood Street Congregation had multiple sources—some vital, some dismissed. Along with his theological education, Brian's *experiences* informed and reformed his convictions of God's presence and leading. The boot camp's religious professionals were dismissed as credible sources for discerning his vision and calling. Brian embraced a former pimp and oppressed persons he met in Atlanta as discernment guides.

What factors keep your heart open to listening for discernment? What in someone's or some institution's history leads you to decide that they have little or nothing to offer your discerning heart? Where do you struggle to be open to God's presence in persons whose identity or faith traditions are different than your own? Are there experiences in your life that cause you to disqualify yourself as a trustworthy source for discernment? How is prayer important to your listening and discernment?

⚜ ⚜ ⚜ ⚜ ⚜ ⚜ ⚜ ⚜

In my teaching, the first day of class has always had a distinctive quality of anticipation and readiness—for both the students and me. We have a fresh start on the semester. The subject matter is new and promising. On this first day, there are no overdue assignments that dampen enthusiasm, no disappointing grades on papers and exams. Students are eager to review the syllabus and dive into the concepts of the course. The syllabus schedule can feel like the design for a race from this first day to finals. Ready, set, go!

I have always felt students' heightened eagerness to move through the course. So, I was enchanted by what students reported to me about the first day in another class they were taking on spirituality. The professor had said, "We will start slow." Of course, this is expected as one is getting oriented to a subject's discipline, before the course ramps up and sprints through the schedule. This professor, however, had had a different description about the pace of instruction for the coming days of the course on spirituality: "We will start slow . . . and then we will go slower."

Going slower is a faithful approach in discernment. Taking time to establish relationships. Connecting with others with contemplative listening. Speaking one's own heart for others to hear. Appreciating the complexity of persons and communities that merit accompaniment instead of seeking a quick fix. *Lingering* with the spirit of God as we *linger* with one another. A slower pace serves our contemplative discernment. Hope is often known only after contemplative time together. *Hope is here in discerning hearts!*

The Engaging Heart

Our engaging hearts beat for enlivening opportunities to become a people for justice and beloved community—opportunities that *transform* us and the world. The opportunities abound. We have no faithful excuse for failing to engage the opportunities that emerge from prayerful listening and discerning.

Failing to engage what we have heard and discerned occurs because of reservations discussed in chapter 2 in "The Hope We Resist": we are complacent in being captives to "the tyranny of the familiar"; with elevated hopefulness to have a creative impact on community, we doubt our ability to withstand disappointing outcomes; and our fear of suffering, especially from pain, overshadows courage to engage. Fear of suffering can be the most difficult problem to overcome. Persons are not only *distracted*, but also *immobilized* by pain. Pain takes hold of us in ways that demand our full attention. So even perceiving the possibility of suffering can forestall engaging what has been heard and discerned in prayer.

The spiritual death knell sounds when we fail to give ourselves to a vital life because we have submitted to the threat of living with pain. The excruciating reality of pain is never to be denied. Avoiding unnecessary pain is wise. What we must avoid is allowing pain to hold us captive to a shrunken life. Our growth comes from engaging our capacities and engaging life.

Taylor Emmaus McGhee is in my "cloud of witnesses" with a testimony about the transformative possibility from listening, discerning, and engaging. Her life speaks to the promise of overcoming *fear of pain and pain itself.* The engaging heart, with hope, has creative purposes to fulfill.

✠ ✠ ✠ ✠ ✠ ✠ ✠

I've known Taylor Emmaus all her life. Even though I had celebrated her birthdays, artistic accomplishments, and graduations, there was so much more I wanted to know about her life journey and her becoming a witness to hope. What in her twenty-two years of life enabled her to engage her chronic illnesses without losing joy and the determination to fulfill her sense of purpose? On whom and what did her authentic self rely to endure pain and disruptive trips to emergency rooms and hospitalizations, be excited by relationships with Tibetan monks, pursue her passion for music, excel in education, and adjust her dreams to the realities of her body?

Taylor Emmaus had always counted on her body to express her deepest feelings—feelings for which words are inadequate. She welcomed dance lessons at age two and became so advanced that she envisioned dance as her future career. A broken arm at six years old did not end her dream of dancing. It began, however, escalating experiences of pain that have persisted throughout her life. Despite pain, she continued to dance and accelerate into classes with the most advanced dancers. At age 15, she began training to audition for dance companies as the next step in her trajectory for becoming a professional dancer. While practicing a lift with a dance partner, she dislocated her hip. Although she sought immediate medical attention for the dislocation and ongoing pain, because a doctor misread the radiology report, it was two years later before other doctors determined that she had also fractured one of her spinal joints.

When told, "You'll never dance again," she was "crushed." She says, "I have such a physical relationship to the world, . . . and to no longer be able to do that [dance] and having to communicate what I was feeling with words was very challenging." Injury was not new for her. She had continued to dance through previous bone breaks. This injury, however, changed the course of her life. In addition to not dancing, the body pain kept her from concentrating on schoolwork. Weakness in ligaments and tendons, multiple dislocations, complex fractures, and broken bones continued. She recalls being "in and out of doctors' offices and the emergency room always with something." In her senior year of high school, after two years of seeing more than forty doctors who concluded that she was clumsy and not attentive to her surroundings, she was finally diagnosed with Ehlers-Danlos syndrome (EDS) type 3 hypermobility. The diagnosis confirmed what she already knew: that at her cautious best in whatever she did, her body continued to weaken. This genetic disease impeded vigorous movement as it continued to give rise to relentless pain, hospitalizations, surgeries, and long recoveries.

In her first year of college, she experienced fainting spells. These occurred when she would move rapidly from sitting to standing or from lying down. Her heart rate soared as her blood pressure dropped. She was diagnosed with postural orthostatic tachycardia syndrome (POTS)—a condition linked to EDS. This diagnosis helped to explain childhood experiences of passing out and becoming easily overheated. While the fainting and injuries from POTS and EDS ended her dream of having a professional dance career, she began to choreograph new physical movements to negotiate basic daily routines.

With all these adversities, I wanted to know what enabled her to dance with hope and be enlivened to life. Since pain and body trauma are not relegated to her past, how does she sustain vitality and hopefulness? When I asked her about this, she attributed her resiliency to three formative experiences. First, the support of her ancestors and their inspiring life stories. They are her witnesses for life. She says, "It was instilled in me from a very young age that who I am today is because of all who have come before me." These ancestors "grounded" her, and she felt an indebtedness to them for this heritage. Speaking from her identity as a biracial (African American and White) woman, she says:

> I had a certain duty to live a better life than my ancestors had led. [I was determined to persist] in order to honor them, and

in order to honor their struggles and their experiences, and to change this intergenerational narrative of trauma and of strife and of grave loss and a lack of belonging. . . . A spiritual encounter takes place when you walk on the land that your ancestors were enslaved on.

The example and consolations received from her father, who also has EDS, have been essential in sustaining her. Because of his own struggles with EDS, his empathy and loving responses carried the authoritative force of "one who knows." The ancestors, living and dead, inspire and nurture.

Second, she was unmoored by the death of her beloved grandfather. Their relationship was so special to her that, when he died, she struggled to believe she could live without his physical presence in her life. She describes his death as "a faith crisis" that intensified her focus on God and on questions of meaning that were "greater than my grief." Working through this unprecedented loss, and the feelings of doubt and anger that accompanied it, she arrived at a place where she felt like "a different person," who was even more determined to live into the future in the exemplary tradition of her heritage. She characterizes her ancestors and family as "an embodied form of hope." Their imprint on her life led her to declare, "I will be the person for my generation to continue that."

Third, her determination to be "an embodied form of hope" is grounded in a more acute awareness of God's presence in her life. Chronic pain, for many people, annihilates their belief in a personal, loving God. Their prayers for relief seem to be uttered into a heartless void. For Taylor Emmaus, God's presence was known. She says, "You learn who God is when you have to learn to walk again." Her statement is one of both letting go and embracing. Letting go of false notions of self-reliance and embracing the abiding love of God and others. EDS and POTS reset the mobility of her body. The embrace of God reset the commitment of her life.

The physical realities were not ignored. She continued in pain. However, "I needed to believe that there was more to living than debilitating pain. . . . I don't want to be cured or to be changed from my experience [of pain]. I want to use that to shape me and mold me into the person that God created me to be." She continues with her illnesses. Still, learning how to walk after her spinal fracture, being fully reliant on other people for the most basic ways of taking care of herself, losing her former sense of independence and agency—all this made her more determined to fulfill God's calling upon her life. She says, "I wasn't learning to walk again for the sake of walking. I was learning to walk again to lead a better life."

Taylor Emmaus's journey has been an emotional roller coaster that has had its times of derailing. Depression and anxiety occurred—conditions that have their own ways of disabling. Again, in recognizing the need for help beyond her capacities, she took medication that (1) enabled her to feel better; (2) helped her understand that her struggle was not because of a spiritual lapse, but that she had a chemical imbalance in her brain; and (3) restored her belief that even from such emotional depths, she had assistance to feel better. The emotional and physical challenges of her past have shaped her outlook for engaging the future. Challenges can decimate us. They are also opportunities to instruct and transform us to experience our authentic selves anew. Regarding forthcoming struggles, she says, "I've transcended them before, so I can do it again. I've learned things along the way. You don't know how strong you really are until you've faced something you could have never imagined."

Taylor Emmaus continues to live with hope and hopefulness. As a self-identified "Black biracial queer woman and disabled person," she gives herself to the blessings and struggles of these identities. They not only constitute her sense of self; each informs her work in becoming. In 2021, she graduated magna cum laude from Emory University with a Bachelor of Arts in Media Studies. Then she completed a Master of Theological Studies, graduating magna cum laude, in which she explored the intersections of youth ministry and queer theology in the Wesleyan/Methodist tradition. Upon graduating from Boston University School of Theology, she was hired to be the director of children, youth, and family ministries at a church in Seattle, Washington. Taylor Emmaus is enlivened to life as she "could have never imagined."

❖ ❖ ❖ ❖ ❖ ❖ ❖ ❖

Every person's journey with chronic pain has its distinctive experiences, lessons, and transformations. Pain can be periodically or always excruciating. Persons can have supporters who comfort, or they can suffer loneliness. Hopefulness comes from faith in God or medicine or self or nothing. Hope's work in these varied experiences is to bring forth vitality and joy for purposeful living. Hope's impact is personal and communal as it abides with sufferers, supporters, medical professionals, and those reticent to become involved. Hope persists to birth us anew.

When the engaging heart encounters pain and illness, more is at stake than discomfort and debilitation. With the witnesses I've known both personally and through accounts of their lives, the greatest fears are of losing a sense of one's authentic self, a sense of purpose, and experiencing life as a joy. Both the Taylor Emmaus McGhee and Reynolds Price (see chapter 1) stories portray the spirit-saving work to address these fears. Their praying hearts *listened* deeply to their authentic selves, the voices of a supportive community (living and dead), the resources of faith, and the presence of God. They *discerned* ways to endure and be empowered for a future worth anticipating. And they *engaged* purposes that responded to what they had heard and discerned.

Engaging hearts honor their prayers for justice and peace through activism for justice and peace. The activism is not only a response to prayer; *activism is prayer*. Rabbi Abraham Joshua Heschel gives testimony to social activism as prayer. Speaking of his 1965 march with Martin Luther King Jr. and other civil rights activists, he says:

> For many of us the march from Selma to Montgomery was both protest and prayer. Legs are not lips, and walking is not kneeling. And yet our legs uttered songs. Even without words, our march was worship. I felt my legs were praying.[6]

In Heschel's marching prayer, he became more alive to his relationship with God and more alive to his relationship with those who suffer injustice. *Listening, discerning, and engaging are a prayer continuum.* The work of hope empowers a prayer that may begin in a prayer closet and continues by protesting at citadels of social injustice.

⚜ ⚜ ⚜ ⚜ ⚜ ⚜ ⚜

Becoming a people for beloved community entails deep listening and discernment in a church's own community. Its community is not only an immediate source for discernment, but also a necessary one. Too often churches will initiate neighborhood outreach programs without consulting neighbors. Food pantries, community gardens, mothers day out/parents day out, after-school mentoring, and vacation Bible schools are launched because of a perceived need. Disappointment follows if these programs fail to attract the expected number of people from the community.

Community members should be involved in a church's discernment about being a caring neighbor. The *invitation* to be involved in the discernment process is itself a statement of valuing neighbors as sources of knowledge and wisdom. As stated in chapter 2, invitations are life changing—for hosts and guests. Hearts are available to one another. An invitation that was conceived as discussing programs turns into conversations about families, personal histories, faith journeys, and hope. Rather than church members deciding what they might do to enrich neighbors' lives, the enrichment experience between church members and neighbors is mutual.

Even if programming emerges from this joint discernment, it may fail to involve the larger community. A major difference in this failure, however, is the appreciation of the church's neighbors for having a voice in the effort rather than being bystanders to a failed outcome. Together, church and community members can grieve a failed effort, celebrate their heart-binding relationship, and pursue new initiatives to benefit their community.

The way forward is marked by companionship rather than paternalistic decision-making. Discernment with neighbors might shift the focus from what a single church can accomplish, to working with community organizations and other churches in the community. A church's identity and understanding of itself may evolve from occupying a neighborhood to being a neighbor. *Hope is here, in the engaging heart!*

✣ ✣ ✣ ✣ ✣ ✣ ✣

Wonderful variations of prayer are available for the diversity of persons, and their diverse temperaments, moods, and conditions. Hope enlivens through all the variations. What most threatens the work of hope, and our assurance of God's presence, is not the failure to adopt a particular gesture for praying. The biggest threat is not even the doubts we may have about prayer itself. What most threatens the work of hope is our failure to keep praying.

In observing Jesus beyond the contemplative settings, his life stresses always living prayerfully. Instructing his disciples about prayer, he tells them to be persistent in prayer (Luke 11:5–10). Prayer is asking, seeking, and knocking as if life depended upon answers being given, things being found, and doors being opened. This is the urgency and tenacity of praying. Prayer enables us to be alive to the promise of each moment as sacred experience with ultimate meaning. Prayer-fulness in "each moment" may seem impossible, but such an attitude toward life has been the intent and achievement of persons for whom prayer has been as necessary and regular as breathing. Another way of expressing this conviction is to say, "May all things be done in the spirit of prayer." Parenting, eating food, cleaning bathrooms, resolving conflicts, sexual intercourse and sexual abstinence, care for the sick, and all matters of living are conducted in the awareness of God's presence and with the desire to be a joy to God's heart.

One of the most celebrated persons to exemplify this disposition was Brother Lawrence—a seventeenth-century Carmelite lay brother. He performed the most menial tasks with the belief that everything is done in the presence of God, and that therefore all actions have the significance of being sacred. In the book of Brother Lawrence's few letters (*The Practice of the Presence of God*), Joseph de Beaufort records a conversation with Brother Lawrence:

> [Brother Lawrence felt] that it was a great delusion to think that the times of prayer ought to differ from other times. . . . That his prayer was nothing but a sense of the presence of God, his soul being at that time insensible to anything but Divine love. That when the appointed times of prayer were past, he found no difference, because he still continued with God, praising and blessing Him with all his might, so that he passed his life in continual joy.[7]

God's presence in every moment of our lives sacralizes every moment of our lives. Our assignment is to do all our work with the awareness that God's presence brings meaning and value to whatever we do and fail to do.

We must be careful to avoid the conclusion that setting aside special time and energy to pray is unnecessary. Entering all activities prayerfully is quite different than being busy and labeling busyness as "prayer." Confusing the two is certain to atrophy one's prayer life. Prayer helps to focus us on what our authentic selves are telling us about our purpose amid daily routines and crises that immobilize.

Even if we have a prayerful attitude about both monumental and mundane matters of our lives, this does not eliminate the significance of contemplative prayer. Jesus serves as an example of this insight. The Gospels present Jesus as having an intense awareness of God's presence in all that he did. Still, the Gospels note that Jesus took the time to go to certain places where he could be alone in prayer (Mark 1:35 and Luke 5:16). The spiritual vitality he exhibited in his ministry was related to the spiritual vitality he received in his contemplative times of prayer.

By analogy, a married couple interacts with the responsibilities of caring for one another and their household. They work, shop, parent, tend to each other during illness, visit friends, and do household chores. With all this, their relationship longs for *something more* as an expression of their love—times when "I love you" is spoken and heard, anniversaries are celebrated, bodies are intimate, and dreams are shared. This "something more" is not a substitute for the stated everyday responsibilities; neither is it superior to them. Both expressions of love are important to sustain the relationship. The "something more" brings distinctive expressions of love that deepen the couple's experiences of one another.

Contemplative praying contributes to our becoming a people for beloved community. Deep listening and discerning in contemplative praying cultivate prayerful listening and discerning when we are in situations rife with urgency, activity, and conflict. Contemplative praying attunes us for all the other times of life. Our authentic selves in frenetic seasons benefit from formation in contemplative grounding.

As we practice the forthcoming spiritual disciplines of *Hope Is Here!*, our experience of contemplative praying informs both our disposition and behaviors. Contemplative praying helps us to *remember prophetically* and emboldens us to engage (enact in our lives) what we have heard and discerned. We listen to our authentic selves and others with greater awareness of our oneness and distinctiveness as we *cross identity boundaries*. Our empathy and creative interaction increase with opponents as we *transform conflict* to experience beloved community. The communion with God in contemplative praying is a heartfelt experience that yearns for fulfillment in *celebrating community*.

An ancient definition of faith is "the heart is in it." Faith is a heart commitment. Who we become "for God's sake" is a heart matter. As with our physical hearts, our spiritual hearts rely upon nurture and exercise. Deep listening, discernment, and engagement are the *needed* nurture and exercise for heart vitality. Hope works through these expressions of contemplative praying to bring forth the authentic self, reveal the Way forward, and empower activism for justice and beloved community. Whatever doubt or certainty we have about "prayer changing things" is answered by praying—praying with the heart in it. May our praying be as persistent as our hearts' need for vitality. *Hope is here in contemplative praying!*

Questing with Questions

1. Among the many questions posed in this chapter, identify one or two that are especially compelling for your ongoing reflection. What makes the question(s) compelling? Consider praying contemplatively about the question(s).
2. Do the prayers—spoken or read—of someone else, living or dead, inspire you? If so, what about their praying moves your heart?
3. Where do you go to have a contemplative time in prayer? What do you take or leave behind so that you are deeply present to this time?
4. When and how do you invite others to join your discerning heart? For what types of prayerful matters do you seek others' counsel?
5. What significance do you give to Scripture, Christian tradition, and personal experience as sources for your discerning?

6. By what criteria do you interpret whether you have discerned correctly?

7. Reflect on a time when prayer was vital to your ability to live hopefully through pain, sickness, anxiety, or grief. To the best of your memory, what was prayer addressing for you during this time?

8. When has prayer led you to engage in an act of compassion and/or justice? What occurred in prayer to inspire you to become involved?

Chapter Four

Prophetic Remembering

> Moses said to the people, "Remember this day on which you
> came out of Egypt, out of the house of slavery, because the
> LORD brought you out from there by strength of hand."
> —Exod. 13:3

> Morally speaking, there is no limit to the concern one must
> feel for the suffering of human beings, that indifference to
> evil is worse than evil itself, that in a free society, some are
> guilty, but all are responsible.
> —Abraham Joshua Heschel, "Reasons for
> My Involvement in the Peace Movement"

Remembering to Remember

Throughout the Bible, remembering is an action for living faithfully
in the present. We are told to "remember the Sabbath day," remember God's commandments, remember our covenants, remember the
law and the prophets, remember the ancestors of the faith, remember
what God has done for us. As Jesus has his last meal with his disciples
before his crucifixion, he takes a loaf of bread, gives thanks to God,
breaks the bread, and gives it to his disciples, saying: "This is my body,
which is given for you. Do this in remembrance of me" (Luke 22:19).

Prophetic remembering is not just recalling past events or commands; it is submission to the authority and meaning of what we

remember. Prophetic remembering is not just an exercise of the mind; it is the commitment of our lives. To remember God's commandments is not just being able to recite them; it is living our lives in faithful response to them. Remembering covenants is not just knowing when they were made and what they say; it is a fundamental commitment to be faithful to our covenantal relationships. Remembering the prophets and ancestors of faith is not about being able to name them to win Bible quizzes; it is submitting our lives to the teaching and example of the prophets and ancestors.

This deeper understanding of remembering is evident in our current relationships. After you have stood in the rain for two hours past the time a friend agreed to pick you up, and you ask, "Did you remember that you said you would be here at noon?" you are not satisfied with the friend saying, "Yes, I remembered," with no explanation or sign of remorse.

At the end of a day that has had no special plans, gifts, or expressions of affection, when a spouse asks, "Did you remember that today is our anniversary?" the sole response, "Yes, I remembered" is not reassuring to the heartfelt question for remembrance. Prophetic remembering enacts a response that honors what is remembered. The last chapter closed with a definition of faith: "The heart is in it." *Prophetic remembering (faithful remembering) has the heart in it.*

In this chapter we discuss prophetic remembering as not just what the Hebrew prophets remembered, but also *their example for how we are to remember.* The prophets remembered what God said and how such a message spoke to their current situation. *The prophets listened and heard God continuing to speak in their times*; and they remembered to proclaim and *enact* God's call for compassion and justice. Our becoming a people for beloved community involves being enlivened by hope to our history and current realities. Our faith relies upon our being deeply rooted in a past where God spoke to our ancestors and their future generations about love and justice. Our faith also relies upon being acutely aware of God calling us *now* to care for those who suffer cruelty and oppression. Each of us can enact the spiritual practice of prophetic remembering. Immediate opportunities abound for individuals and churches to *be prophetic* and to embody what God has revealed. Beloved community occurs and is sustained by the God-inspired commitment to personal and systemic *prophetic neighboring*. Such a prophetic commitment is true to the prophetic role of *remembering the future*. This chapter invites us to embrace not just the title of being a prophetic people but also the opportunities to remember prophetically in our activism with hope.

✤✤✤✤✤✤✤

The past is a place of meeting. History awaits us. Yes, we arrive with curiosity and questions and judgment. In addition, we desire to arrive with an eagerness to *listen* for the lessons and yearnings that will contribute creatively to our time. Some lessons, like "to everything there is a season," come easily. Some yearnings, like the desire for freedom, come intensely. However, many lessons and yearnings are not easily or intensely evident. We see the carnage of war and yet continue to marshal military might as a first solution to conflict. Our pronouncements about the inherent value of every person get modified if the person is incarcerated or a political adversary or someone who challenges cultural norms. Vigilance as denizens and interpreters of the past is crucial to prophetic remembering. Without the commitment to perceive the work of hope in history, we are left with *pathetic remembering* rather than prophetic remembering.

The prophet Micah records God pleading with Israel to remember the liberating and saving acts that God has done for the people (Mic. 6:1–5). In an effort to assuage God's anger, the prophet asks, "With what shall I come before the LORD and bow myself before God on high?" Possible sacrifices are suggested by the questioner: "burnt offerings, with calves a year old?" To address the critical situation of God's displeasure, extreme offerings are then named to test what, if anything, can satisfy God: "Will the LORD be pleased with thousands of rams, with ten thousands of rivers of oil? Shall I give my firstborn for my transgression, the fruit of my body for the sin of my soul?" These questions ask, What can we do? The answer is, Remember what God has *already* told you: "to do justice and to love kindness and to walk humbly with your God" (Mic. 6:6–8). What is needed is available; remembering is a fundamental act of faithfulness.

Jesus tells a parable about a rich man whose life is given over to sumptuous living. Living close to the rich man is Lazarus, who suffers from abject poverty. After their deaths, Lazarus is carried by angels to be with Abraham, and the rich man is tormented in Hades. When the rich man looks up and sees Abraham, he begs Abraham to send Lazarus to ease his torment. When Abraham declares that traversing the chasm between them is impossible, the rich man asks Abraham to send Lazarus to warn the rich man's five brothers about the horrendous future that awaits them if they continue their ways. Abraham replies, "They have Moses and the prophets; they should listen to them." In other words, what will save them has already been given to them; they just need to remember and abide by what they hear. The rich man is certain that Abraham's answer is insufficient and insists, "If someone from the dead goes to them, they will repent." To this Abraham responds, "If they do not listen to Moses and the prophets, neither will they be convinced even if someone rises from the dead" (Luke 16:19–31). The parable is clear about the damning consequences from failing to remember what God has already provided. Prophetic lives have given us instruction through their speaking and witness. To fail to remember them and abide by their God-given guidance is to ignore God.

✤ ✤ ✤ ✤ ✤ ✤ ✤

I live five miles from Stone Mountain Park. The 3200 acres are publicized as Georgia's most-visited attraction. With beautiful hiking trails through forests, lake views, recreational attractions, golf courses, a simulated village for eating and souvenirs, festivals, and other appealing features for locals and tourists, the park is a popular destination. Every time I enter the park, I'm inspired by its beauty and the images of people enjoying its offerings and one another. And also on each visit, I'm troubled by the park's identity as a tribute to the Confederacy.

The purchase of the land and its development are tied to the United Daughters of the Confederacy and the Ku Klux Klan. The park's "mountain," rising 825 feet above surrounding terrain, is described as "the world's largest piece of exposed granite." You can either walk or ride a cable-car skyride to the top. The summit provides an unobstructed 360-degree view of the horizon. Visually and recreationally, the mountain is the park's defining feature. Its massive carving (considered the "largest relief structure in the world") of three Confederate leaders is a "must see" for the best unobstructed view of the mountain.

The museum, exhibit hall, and film presentations focus on the Civil War and the Confederacy. The park's streets are named for the Confederate president and two Confederate generals. Except for a reproduction of a slave plantation, the horrors of slavery and the significance of slavery in the rise of the Confederacy are absent.

I'm offended that a narrative about the Confederacy basically ignores a primary cause for the Civil War—the effort to preserve the enslavement of Black people. Throughout the park is the celebration of the Confederacy and the heroism of its defenders. Throughout the park the inhumane "way of life" for which the Confederacy fought is largely ignored. I am not opposed to telling the story of the Confederacy with attention to its victories and tragic losses. However, a narrative that excludes the cruel reality of slavery that the Confederacy defended invalidates the Park's significance for prophetic remembering.

Omissions foster forgetting, and forgetting is often an intentional way to misinterpret the past. Turkey's official denial of the genocide of approximately one million Armenians during World War I, persons who deny that six million Jews died in the Holocaust, the failure of American history textbooks to mention the United States government's breaking treaties with indigenous nations (Native Americans), and so many other examples are evidence of efforts to forget.

Adam Hochschild's *King Leopold's Ghost* is a remarkable account of Belgium's King Leopold II's takeover of the Congo in 1885. His nearly-twenty-five-year reign over the Congo is a story of torture, mutilations, slave labor, slaughter (estimated at over ten million people), and ecological rape on a massive scale. Just before Leopold transferred the land from his private ownership to Belgium as a colony, Leopold ordered the burning of all archives related to his administration of the Congo. Regarding "the politics of forgetting," Hochschild writes, "The furnaces burned for eight days, turning most of the Congo state records to ash and smoke in the sky over

Brussels. 'I will give them my Congo,' Leopold told Stinglhamber [a military aide], 'but they have no right to know what I did there.'"[1] This forgetting was not a failure in memory; this forgetting was an intentional effort to erase what was remembered.

We inherit intentional and systemic efforts to forget. James W. Loewen's *Lies My Teacher Told Me* forensically details how high-school American history textbooks omit and distort historical events in order to appease textbook review boards of school systems. These boards, politicians, and many vocal parents want an historical narrative that emphasizes the virtues of the nation and minimizes its failings. Loewen concludes that generations of high-school students have received a mythological history of a "U.S. government that deserves students' allegiance, not their criticism."[2] Regardless of course grades, a false history fails the students and the nation. We then have citizens, formed by distorted lessons about the past, who are unable to correctly interpret the causes of current social conflicts and crises.

Public education's systemic forgetting and minimizing of embarrassing realities in the nation's history undermine prophetic remembering. In addition to diminishing the lessons to be learned from abhorrent customs and laws, we are denied the inspiring narratives of persons who fought against these laws and customs. The commitment of abolitionists, organizers for safe labor conditions, advocates for women's right to vote, those who protested Japanese internment camps during World War II, and so many more who responded prophetically against injustice need to be highlighted and remembered. They are exemplary for the prophetic formation of children and adults. The significance and instruction from their witness occurs only if the realities they confronted are truthfully portrayed.

Remembering is essential for engaging current and coming realities with the power of truth and courageous witness. If we embrace a false past, we eventually embody it. Our capacity to be a people for beloved community is diminished. God's dream for beloved community is revealed in history—through achievements and tragedy. We must therefore devote ourselves to the sacred task of remembering the past as fully and honestly as possible. *Hope is here to enliven us to the lessons of history!*

Being Prophetic

Prophetic remembering is not just about remembering biblical prophets. All of us are called to live and remember prophetically. *God remembers us* and is constant with presence, love, and hope. Responding faithfully to whatever God has made manifest in the relationship with us is our prophetic role.

Returning to the Scripture from Micah, we have guidance to the question, "What does the Lord require of us?" We live and remember prophetically when we "do justice." The requirement is far beyond not being unjust. Avoiding culpability in treating others unjustly is good. However, it can also result in passive responses to injustice. The holy command to "do justice" calls us *to act to bring forth justice in our relationships and throughout God's land.* Micah rails against seizing people's property and depriving them of means to flourish. The oppression being experienced leaves people desperate and desolate. The culprits are devious rulers, self-serving priests, and false prophets—in other words, those in official positions of authority and power. Doing justice involves engaging the powers and principalities that perpetrate injustice. This also entails protesting the policies, laws, and institutions that perpetuate systemic injustice—whether or not we had anything to do in creating and supporting them.

The text is not focused on "What does the Lord require of Micah?" but on "What does the Lord require of *us*?" We do justice by honoring the rights of others and by opposing those who oppress. Indifference and passivity to cruelty and injustice are not prophetic options. God's dream of beloved community requires prophetic activism. Becoming a people for beloved community is to be prophetic.

※ ※ ※ ※ ※ ※ ※

The past and present are stages for the dramas that shape our identities and purposes. Interpreting the dramas of history and God's actions has never had only one narrative. Interpreters contend with one another. A characterization of university faculty as "those who think otherwise" is both amusing and accurate. Academic reputations rise and fall on contentious scholarship. Fierce arguments about the most reliable interpretations of the past are not confined to the academy. Contentious interpretations of God's action in history (including Scriptures) have led to church schisms, heresy accusations, torture, and death. Interpreting is consequential!

Prophets interpret. Being prophetic entails perceiving how God is active in these dramas and announcing how our behaviors betray or agree with what God desires. All of us, in our prophetic remembering, are to prepare ourselves to interpret soundly. A prophetic people are stewards of the past, with the responsibility to guard it against distortions that pervert its lessons. Without our stewardship, the past is left in the control of others whose primary concerns may ignore how hope enlivens for justice and beloved community. What then do we remember about the work of hope when we travel to the past? A past without faithful and skilled stewards may be a past unworthy of remembrance.

I continue to hear reactionary media personalities and citizens who oppose focusing on racism quote Martin Luther King Jr's phrase, "I have a dream that my four little children will one day live in a nation where they will not be judged by the color of their skin but by the content of their character." These interpreters assert that King would be against public education teaching children about the atrocity of slavery and its consequences. They characterize King as being opposed to affirmative action initiatives and protests emphasizing racial disparities. Their remaking of King in their own image presents him as uninterested in all matters about race. They hijack and corrupt his prophetic message. When faithful stewards insist on truthful portrayals of prophets, the stewards sustain hope's work to enliven a prophetic people.

In our commitment to being stewards of the past, we often face competing versions of history that seem credible. Our diligence as stewards does not result in having indisputable interpretations of our history. Stewardship, however, must be faithful to the pursuit of truth, though uncertainty persists. Certitude, rather than doubt, is more often the bane for seeking truth. Stewards avail themselves with the best-known means to discern truth and to defend against errors.

Trustworthy interpretation involves study. The process of seeking truth yields insight and meaning. We hope it also yields humility about the insights and meanings. Rabbi Abraham Joshua Heschel, in writing about "the essence of Judaism," stresses "the centrality of the act" when stating, "The act of studying is more important than the possession of knowledge."[3] The pursuit of truth is formative; it forms us as a prophetic people. Even when today's conclusions are revised years later, the act of study continually opens our minds and hearts to experience God anew. Study is a means for walking humbly with God.

The journey into the past through study encounters our faith ancestors. Their witness instructs and encourages us. The ancestors enhance our interpretive capacities. In the Gospels, we hear Jesus referring to his tradition of history, laws, and prophets. Tradition is a means for being rooted in the fertile ground of ancestral experience, wisdom, and example. Study and discernment are then informed by centuries of trustworthy witnesses of faith. G. K. Chesterton argued the importance of tradition to understanding faith:

> Tradition means giving votes to the most obscure of all classes, our ancestors. It is the democracy of the dead. Tradition refuses to submit to the small and arrogant oligarchy of those who merely happen to be walking about. . . . Tradition objects to [the ancestors] being disqualified by the accident of death.[4]

The ancestors are vital to our prophetic work of interpretation and stewardship.

Being prophetic also entails remembering that God calls us *now*. Divine encounters are not relegated to the past. As stewards of the present, we interpret where cruelty and injustice reign. The violations we see grip our hearts, and *we know* we are called to respond with our lives. Yes, in our awareness of the violations, we will identify organizations and persons whose current prophetic engagement inspires us. They merit recognition as prophetic witnesses in our midst. *We are called to join them as prophetic witnesses.* Prophetic remembering entails remembering that God has called us to be prophetic now.

The Hebrew prophets' messages for justice and compassion inspire and disturb us. We confront responsibilities that disrupt the status quo—in society, in the church, and in our lives. As described in chapter 2, we often resist hope when it involves overcoming *the tyranny of the familiar.* More than simply requiring us to marshal energies to change routines and relationships, overcoming this tyranny also confronts us with the hostility of friends, strangers, church members, and officials who fear the transformations. Being prophetic risks reactions that condemn and threaten.

Being prophetic can also enliven us to God and life in extraordinary ways. Our true selves shine forth. Purpose is clear. Meaning comforts and guides us. We reside in emotions of freedom and hopefulness. These joyful experiences occur even with prophetic persons who continue to be ostracized, shunned, and incarcerated. Serving faithfully does not prevent us from being grief stricken as we lament ongoing indifference and injustice. Heartache and heartbreak persist. Still, prophetic commitment is so aligned with hope that a fuller sense of God-given identity, vocation, and joy prevails amid our travails.

As stated in Micah, crucial to being an embodied messenger of God's desire for beloved community is to "walk humbly with God." Cultivating humility is the antidote to persons believing they are God's only messengers and that they have all the answers. In the biblical Scriptures, God warns, God laments, God desires, God acts, and God is the source of salvation. A prophet's role is to receive God's message and to announce it. Speaking God's message is an awesome responsibility that often evokes self-doubt about one's worthiness to have such a role. Moses believes his lack of eloquence disqualifies him for the role. Isaiah confesses to being a man of "unclean lips." The prophets' deficiencies do not cancel the roles that *God has chosen* for them. Being prophetic occurs when God chooses and persons accept (even reluctantly). We are wise to go forth with God humbly by respecting that God authorizes and empowers whatever constitutes our being prophetic. Walking humbly with God enables prophets to hear clearly and respond faithfully.

Even when the message of compassion and justice is certain, how God directs prophetic action is changeable. Jonah complains, sulks, and asks to die because God's mind changes after the people of Nineveh repent (Jonah 3–4). Despite our certainty about what God will do or what God should do, God has the freedom to change. Continuing to act prophetically involves being openhearted in our relationship with God. As stressed in chapter 3, prayer is an essential spiritual discipline for this relationship in our effort to listen, discern, and engage faithfully. To walk humbly with God is to communicate prayerfully with God.

Humility also helps us recognize the complexity of persons and circumstances, although we are certain about God's urgent call for compassion and justice. God's call to prophetic activism may require us to be alert to many fluid realities. What experts and authorities are available to explain our justice issue? What training prepares us to be effective advocates? Considering the multiplicity of social media, where should announcements of issues and actions be given? With whom do we need to align to be effective? Since social transformation often depends on a strategic sequence of actions, how do we get the timing right? How do we sustain our activism over the years required to accomplish successful outcomes? These *basic* questions are integral to the response of doing justice. Being prophetic embraces both the call and the *process* to "do justice." Walking humbly with God releases us from feeling that our prophetic work is dependent upon our own wisdom, patience, and strength. Other people walk humbly with God and are potential companions in our being prophetic. Together we pray, and listen, and discern, and engage, and remember, and study, and serve, and weep, and rejoice, and celebrate. Hope enlivens us to walk humbly with God and companions so that we do "not grow weary in doing what is right" (Gal. 6:9). *Hope is here in being prophetic!*

Prophetic Neighboring

In the Gospel of Luke (chap. 10), a lawyer tests Jesus with the question, "What must I do to inherit eternal life?" Jesus responds by asking the lawyer what he *remembers* from the written law. The lawyer then recites passages from Deuteronomy and Leviticus: "You shall love the Lord your God with all your heart and with all your soul and with all your strength and with all your mind and your neighbor as yourself." Jesus affirms how the lawyer has remembered and directs him, "Do this, and you will live."

The lawyer's intent to test Jesus' authority is also in his second question, "And who is my neighbor?" Regardless of the lawyer's intent, the question reflects the unsettled debate on who merits the status of being a "neighbor." Jesus answers the question with the revealing power of story. He describes how a traveler was robbed, beaten, and left dying. When a priest and later a Levite saw the man, both distanced themselves from him and continued on their way. When a Samaritan saw him, however, the Samaritan took extraordinary measures to care immediately for the man's injuries and to take him to a place where he paid for the man's long-term care.

Jesus asks the lawyer, "Which of these three, do you think, was a neighbor to the man who fell into the hands of the robbers?" The lawyer acknowledges that the neighbor was "the one who showed him mercy." Jesus responds, "Go and do likewise" (Luke 10:25–37). The fact that the Samaritan was the one who merited being the "neighbor" was a shocking twist in the story for the lawyer and other Jewish listeners. Jews believed Samaritans to be religiously reprehensible and ritually unclean. The parable's lesson on the meaning of "neighbor" threw into disarray long-held beliefs about the social order, acceptable relationships, and true religion. Jesus had assaulted *the tyranny of the familiar.*

Despite the clarity of the parable, Christian churches often avoid or have muddled responses to the question, "And who is my neighbor?" Sermons and Sunday school lessons on this Scripture will stress the need to expand our understanding of who qualifies as a neighbor, while ignoring the implications of this question within their church's own communities. In my consultations with churches, I will ask, "How would you describe your relationship with neighbors?" Almost always a long period of silence follows. When discussion starts, the most common responses are these: "Most of our members do not live in the neighborhood." "The residents of the community do not reflect the backgrounds of our members." "Most people in this neighborhood are members of another church, or another religion, or have no interest in joining a church." "People in this community have overscheduled lives with no time for adding another interaction." The responses to my question indicate how church members often think of *relating to neighbors* as contingent upon the likelihood that neighbors will become members, or participate in a church's programs, or have immediate resonance with the church's members.

Behind most of these responses is their weighing the prospects for neighbors to benefit church growth.

The definition of neighbor is especially evident with churches in urban areas that mention the challenge of dealing with the "problem" of homeless persons in their neighborhood and around the church. Those who are residents or have businesses are considered neighbors. Homeless persons are perceived as "outsiders" intruding upon the neighborhood, even though their days and nights are lived in the neighborhood. The biblical command to love our neighbors is not limited to "our kind of people."

Jesus' parable is often cited to indicate that being a neighbor is not determined by proximity. The love God expects us to have for one another is not limited to persons close enough for regular interaction. Equally true, however, is that the proximity of persons does not exclude them from being neighbors who merit the attention of our hearts. Neighbors surround us.

The parable expands the understanding of who is a neighbor, and *it depicts what neighbors do.* A neighborly act is a caring act. Neighbors respond to those they know and to strangers with love. This dimension of the parable must not be lost. Alongside the expanded understanding of who is a neighbor, Jesus says, "Go and [love like a neighbor]."

In my consultations with local churches, the most extended silence comes after I ask, *"How would the people of your community describe your church as a neighbor? What loving acts would they name as their experience of your church?"* The silence speaks uncertainty and, to a large degree, the certainty of embarrassment. What is your response to these questions? How do you anticipate the members of your church answering these questions? What thoughts and feelings do you have about the answers?

Being a prophetic neighbor entails the prophetic role of compassion and doing justice. Responding to neighbors' crises and addressing systemic injustices that oppress them is prophetic work. We must remember, however, that *an essential dimension of being prophetic is relationship with the people.* Prophets walk among the people and hear their anguish. Even when a biblical prophet comes from another part of the country, the prophet knows the people's plight through being with the people. Relationships matter.

In a previous writing, I stress the significance of attending to relationship as a fundamental phase of prophetic neighboring. I cite it here to indicate how individuals and congregations might overcome the alienation that exists between a church and its community. This is a crucial aspect of prophetic activism:

> *Prophetic neighboring* occurs from caring relationship. A congregation need not wait for a crisis or catastrophe to happen before it relates with neighbors. To wait would suggest that neighboring is only a response to someone's problems or weakness. A caring neighbor seeks to be in relationship because the relationship itself is valued. Conversations occur that do not necessarily result in decision-making or action. Rapport is established without the need to have a political agenda. . . .
>
> Neighboring only in crisis suggests that one is solely responsive to another's inabilities. Being a constant neighbor provides more opportunities to experience and appreciate the whole person. A neighbor who has tarried with the heart of another during normal times is more likely to know how to care during crisis.[5]

Prophetic neighboring transforms the church as well as the community. Members experience new relationships that deepen their commitment to the church's identity as a neighbor. The relationships with residents, homeless persons, business owners, other religious leaders, political representatives, and education officials change church members' perspective of the community as just a place *to drive through* to arrive at the place (church) where they are enlivened to life. The community itself becomes a place of enlivening. God waits for us to arrive in the community where God has so much to reveal.

✤ ✤ ✤ ✤ ✤ ✤ ✤ ✤

On a hot Chicago summer evening, and with his church without air conditioning, the Rev. Marvin Frank Thomas Sr. decided to wait outside for members to arrive for Bible study. A young woman walking past the church spoke a greeting, soon turned around, and approached him with a question: "Is this church open?" Rev. Thomas answered, "Yes," but he also heard the question as an indictment.

The "openness" of Walls Memorial Christian Methodist Episcopal Church was not obvious.

Remembering that evening, Rev. Thomas says, "I could not wait for Bible study to start so that I could share the young woman's question with those gathered." The question heard as an indictment inspired a challenge. He repeated the encounter to the Bible study group and said, "The question shall never be asked of this church again!" The *question* sparked a *quest* to have a Christian witness that was known and felt by neighbors.

Later that year, on a cold November morning, he received a call from the church's Missionary Society president to leave his home and give remarks to the missionaries before they ended their monthly meeting. The missionaries had completed their sumptuous breakfast, a two-hour meeting, and were now only waiting to receive his remarks. For an unknown reason, he chose an indirect route to the church that placed him at a stop sign a block from Walls Memorial. While there, he noticed persons warming themselves from the fire in a barrel. After arriving at the church, the image of persons huddled around the barrel remained vivid and inspired him to ask a question to the gathered missionaries:

> When you leave here today, and after you have feasted as you have and had your missionary meeting, you'll get in your cars and drive away on Sacramento Blvd [the street on which Walls Memorial is located]. I wonder what would be your answer to the question, "Will Sacramento Blvd be any better because the missionaries of Walls Memorial have been here feasting?" It seems to me that just on one of your Saturday meetings, instead of feeding yourselves, you would go down to the alley where persons are on the margins of life and warming themselves and invite them to come here and you feed them.

The next morning, the missionary president came to him and said, "Pastor, the missionaries take the challenge. We're going into the alley next month and we are going to get the people and bring them to the church." True to her word, the elderly women drove, and the younger ones walked, about 150 yards to invite those in the alley to Sunday-morning breakfast at the church. After doing this once, the missionary president said, "We've decided that we're going to do this every Sunday."

The Sunday feeding program grew to over three hundred persons—70 percent of whom were guests from the local homeless shelters and the neighborhood. The others were church members. Soon, other organizations of the church were involved in preparing and serving breakfast. Reflecting on the launch and sustenance of this ministry, Rev. Thomas says that although there was no planning and budget, "We never asked the congregation for a dime for the breakfast ministry, but somehow it worked!"

Six months after starting the breakfast ministry, they worked with a city program to start a shelter ministry that fed and housed seventy homeless men each night (7:00 p.m. to 6:30 a.m.). Regarding the meal, Rev. Thomas proudly says, "We did not want this to be a soup and sandwich place. For example, the missionaries were responsible for Monday night's dinner. They served baked chicken, vegetables, peach cobbler—a meal you would get from your grandmother's house." Again, the various church organizations and supportive neighbors chose a night to be certain that full meals were served for every night of the week. Rev. Thomas describes the shelter and breakfast ministries as "a ministry of hospitality and receiving persons not as strangers but as friends and guests who may be experiencing difficulties in life."

The shelter ministry that began for 180 days of refuge from Chicago winter weather soon operated for 365 days a year. Members became aware that cold weather was not the only cause of suffering for those who are homeless. Having a nutritious meal, the opportunity to shower, a safe place to sleep, a mailing address, and caring relationships were basic needs of those who had become their friends.

True to the generative nature of love, more compassion opportunities occurred. On two days a week, the Circle City Health Services brought a team of doctors and other medical professionals to the church to address the medical needs of those who were homeless. If their health problems required additional medical attention, the homeless men would be given a referral—for example, to an optometrist, dentist, or mental health specialist.

Rev. Thomas's involvement with the shelter's external funders led to his becoming president of The Partnership to End Homelessness's board of directors. The organization was a coalition of agencies, community groups, faith communities, businesses, and individuals that addressed the systemic factors that caused and perpetuated homelessness.

The Illinois Department of Corrections designated Walls Memorial's shelter as the official address for men being released from prison who did not have a residence to which they could return. The department had been releasing many parolees to the church's zip code; consequently, a high concentration of formerly incarcerated men were already in the community. The agreement with Walls Memorial's shelter gave some parolees the address they needed for release until they could see their parole officer.

As remarkable as the transformations in the lives of those who were homeless and formerly incarcerated, Walls Memorial itself was being enlivened to life. Members felt more faithful to Jesus' insistence to care for those in need. They were enacting the inspiring messages of Scriptures and sermons. Rev. Thomas reports seeing a new spirit of community within the church, because the members were working together for a bigger purpose than their church's traditional programs. He says that before becoming active in their outreach ministries, the members "knew each other's names, but they did not know each other." The love that motivated their outreach to neighbors was also disclosing their hearts to one another.

The character of the congregation changed. Rev. Thomas describes the congregation of about 180 attending members as a "primarily working-class congregation" in a "working-class neighborhood." The new ministries led some of the homeless men to join the church, participate in the choirs (especially the male chorus), be active in Sunday school and worship, attend Bible study, operate the stairway lift chair for disabled members, and at times help carry caskets up and down stairs for funerals. Members who had retired from their jobs found a new sense of purpose for their lives in the breakfast and shelter ministries. Openheartedness expanded through the ministries. In addressing the tense and difficult situations that occur in caring for persons in traumatizing conditions, Rev. Thomas says, "Even if the people we served had an attitude, we tried to rise above it, and understand the context out of which that comes." Relationships deepened throughout the church.

Over the years since I was a guest preacher at Walls Memorial, I have been inspired by remembering its prophetic neighboring. The opportunity to interview Rev. Thomas (now Bishop Marvin Frank Thomas Sr.) and hear again its story enlivens me. Walls Memorial is a testimony to prophetic remembering and its transformative significance to hope. Being prophetic transforms and empowers—both the prophetic activists and those for whom they care. Relationships that may have started as "giver-to-receiver" transformed into mutual expressions of love and gratitude. Walls Memorial became a vision and lived experience of beloved community. I suspect that consciously or unconsciously, remembering the Scriptures and sermons and Sunday school lessons and prayers led members to remember their baptismal vows. Their past was a vital source for their becoming. Rev. Thomas's closing comment in our interview reflects how prophetic neighboring has an enlivening impact beyond its immediate season. He says, "The story [of Walls Memorial] never gets old and never goes away for me."

❀ ❀ ❀ ❀ ❀ ❀ ❀

Prophets speak God's vision of beloved community. The vision inspires and depicts what hope enlivens us to experience. After his baptism and wilderness ordeal, Jesus went to a synagogue in Nazareth. When given a scroll of the prophet Isaiah, he chose to read a passage that announced his own ministry's prophetic work:

> "The Spirit of the Lord is upon me,
>   because he has anointed me
>   to bring good news to the poor.
> He has sent me to proclaim release to the captives
>   and recovery of sight to the blind,
>   to set free those who are oppressed,
>   to proclaim the year of the Lord's favor."
>
>   (Luke 4:18–19)

The prophetic remembering of Isaiah inspired Jesus.

Jesus' remembering was well received by those in the synagogue until he spoke about God's blessings being extended beyond the people of Israel. Prophetic messages were welcomed when people heard the messages as affirming that God favored them. Hearers were insulted by messages that left them feeling judged or less favored by God. The insult was so severe to Jesus' hearers that they were "filled with rage" and tried to "hurl him off the cliff" (Luke 4:20–30). I wonder how many preachers have envisioned their death as a possible outcome from their first sermons!

Being prophetic is disturbing and disruptive to the status quo. Good news to those who are poor and oppressed is heard as threatening dislocation by others. Trauma and death risks come with being prophetic. We are wise to recognize these possibilities as we continue prophetic activism. Being naive about repercussions can make us unnecessarily vulnerable to being blindsided and defeated. Prophets sometimes become martyrs; however, this is not the goal of being prophetic. Whatever the length of the journey, prophets seek to please God.

Our covenantal relationship with God involves *remembering* God's passion for compassion and justice. Forgetting to be the prophetic people whom God has called us to be is not a faithful option. Yet too many faith communities are prone to forget or ignore what "God requires of us." The Bible speaks persistently about compassionate care for those who are poor and justice for those who are oppressed. These covenantal obligations may be topics of Sunday school lessons and sermons, but prophetic neighboring seldom results. The inaction of churches reflects their failure to submit to what they have heard. How ironic that churches can be passive in remembering Scriptures on justice and care for those who are poor, yet avid activists in remembering the biblical injunctions to worship, pray, and tithe.

Many factors are candidates for this irony. I note five prominent ones that explain, either singularly or in combination, the failure to be prophetic. One is a church's ecclesiology (theological understanding of the church) that does not consider care for cultural realities to be a church purpose. Church is understood as a refuge from culture—a place where persons can pursue their faith without the distractions of societal obligations and crises. The church's mission is defined as preaching, spiritual formation, pastoral care, being a light to the world, and saving souls. Church members may have direct involvement in cultural matters; however, the church does not.

A second explanation is a church's history that does not include prophetic neighboring. The week-by-week and year-by-year life of a local church often reflects traditions established as far back as congregants recall. If prophetic neighboring has not been part of that remembered history, it's less likely to emerge in church planning. "We have always done it this way" is the answer to questions about current and forthcoming scheduling.

The personalities of clergy and lay leadership are a third explanation. Local church leadership that is uncomfortable with their church being involved in social issues will resist prophetic neighboring. Anxiety about involvement with community conflict and issues causing division within the congregation drives their resistance. While it may require considerable effort to initiate a prophetic ministry, church leaders can easily impede endeavors for prophetic neighboring by raising doubts about congregational support, imagining scenarios filled with problems, and naming other priorities needing attention.

A fourth factor relates to churches as religious institutions. Churches affiliated with denominational structures and polity, and even unaffiliated churches organized under procedures, principles, and historic traditions, have status as major institutions in society. They are sources of identity, support, and growth for people in their communities. Along with other social institutions, survival is primary. When prophetic ministry is perceived as irrelevant to survival or as a threat to survival, it garners little interest from church leaders.

And fifth, prophetic ministry frightens church members and leaders. Becoming involved with persons who suffer trauma and injustice is an engagement for which churches feel unprepared. Accompanying the lack of preparation are feelings of incapacity and fear, and disinterest in overcoming incapacity and fear.

Explanations for ignoring prophetic witness are not justifications. The prophet Amos warned Israel about its failure to address the needs of those who are poor and injustices throughout the land. Extravagant religious ceremonies, inspiring choirs, pious speaking, and overflowing attendance do not compensate for inaction on behalf of those who are poor and oppressed. In fact, they only add to the anger God feels from their failure to remember what God has commanded time and time again. God says:

> I hate, I despise your festivals,
>   and I take no delight in your solemn assemblies.
> Even though you offer me your burnt offerings and grain offerings,
>   I will not accept them,
> and the offerings of well-being of your fatted animals
>   I will not look upon.
> Take away from me the noise of your songs;
>   I will not listen to the melody of your harps.
> But let justice roll down like water
>   and righteousness like an ever-flowing stream.
>
> (Amos 5:21–24)

We must remember that *God is always remembering our response-ability* to be compassionate with those who are poor and oppressed. God's dream of beloved community relies upon such prophetic remembering. *Hope is here in prophetic neighboring!*

Remembering the Future

The phrase "remembering the future" sounds like a paradox. Remembering is most always connected with something in the past. Remembering, however, occurs for all dimensions of time. The prophets understood how past and current oppressive realities bespeak a despairing future. The cruel conditions of the people were not acceptable to God. Internal rebellion was not going to be the only consequence. Foreign invaders would control, corrupt, and exile. The prophets remembered what God requires, and they saw how forgetting and ignoring God's heart would result in a dystopian future.

The narratives of these prophetic scriptures declare God acting to bring the terrible outcomes. God's anger sets in motion one destructive event after another. Scholars debate whether prophets know these outcomes because of an ecstatic vision or because coming disasters are the logical result of current misdeeds. Either way, *current* responses to God's requirements shape the future. Indifference to God's commandments and covenants will result in tomorrows full of turmoil and oppression. Remembering this correlation is crucial to having a future worth anticipating.

❧ ❧ ❧ ❧ ❧ ❧ ❧

Envisioning a future that is not just "more of the current anguish" can move persons from hopelessness to transformative behaviors. For example, parents and counselors endeavor to assure children that the bullying they now experience will not last forever. When their children live in fear and humiliation, many sink into depression, and some choose suicide rather than face another day of threat. The day-to-day stress children feel from bullying makes intervention from parents, peers, and schools possibly a matter of life or death. Helping children to envision a future that is not what they now experience can be essential to their hopefulness and recovery from the trauma. Stretching out their sense of time beyond today can help them see new realities that the future offers.

Remembering the future is an action of healing for society's crises. In 1980, Candace Lightner formed Mothers Against Drunk Driving (MADD) after her daughter Cari was killed by a drunk driver. Outraged that drunk drivers, even when they caused fatal accidents, rarely received much punishment from the justice system, Candace Lightner was determined to have her daughter's death change indifference to drunk driving and its tragic consequences on the part of society and the criminal justice system. Cindi Lamb, whose five-month-old daughter, Laura Lamb, had become a quadriplegic because of a drunk driver, soon joined her.

Others joined their campaign to change the laws that failed to punish drunk drivers. But they also wanted to enact laws and increase public awareness to deter drunk driving. Within four years MADD had achieved a Presidential Commission on Drunk Driving, 330 MADD chapters in forty-seven states, an increased minimum-drinking-age law, and 129 new laws against drunk driving. Subsequent years continued with accomplishments that helped society see drunk driving as a crisis for everyone.

MADD became an organization in which thousands of persons whose family members and friends were killed or injured by a drunk driver could respond creatively to their anger and grief. By *preventing* the escalation of drunk-driving accidents, it provided them the opportunity to make a difference. Their remembering the future made the roads safer for everyone.

⚜ ⚜ ⚜ ⚜ ⚜ ⚜ ⚜

I met Dorothy Johnson-Speight, who organized Mothers in Charge after her twenty-four-year-old son (Khaaliq Jabbar Johnson) was killed over a parking space dispute. She spoke of her work to prevent other families from experiencing the pain and heartbreak that comes from the death of a child due to violence. Working with other women in Philadelphia, the organization fought for violence prevention programs, mentoring of youth, grief support for youth whose family and friends had been killed by violence, and legislation for safer communities. Her work on behalf of a less violent and grief-stricken future is a healing response to her loss. Mothers in Charge affiliates have been established in ten US cities. As Dorothy Johnson-Speight remembers her son, she remembers the future.

Returning to Adam Hochschild's disclosures on King Leopold's efforts to eliminate records of the horrors perpetrated in the Belgian Congo, we have another example of how remembering the future is vital to prophetic remembering. In remembering the past, Hochschild does not want us to forget the depths of human depravity in service to greed and power. He also wants us to understand that current problems in the Congo region are related to a traumatized history that involves European invaders and collaborators. Pursuing a more creative future in the Congo needs to be informed by understanding and addressing the generational trauma that continues to haunt the land.

We are indebted to those in the past who remembered the future. Parents, teachers, clergy, civil-rights activists, benefactors to schools, environmentalists, and myriad others who anticipated our coming days labored for us to have nurturing contexts and opportunities. Hope enlivened them to remember a time that waits to exist.

In remembering the future, we can be time-travelers to coming times when our current trauma and oppression are relieved. Today's efforts are essential for taking us to futures with greater promise of awakening us to life's fullness. Our activism is not only on our own behalf, but also for persons and societies mired in the present without an image of a future worth anticipating. Hope awaits us in the future. Hope is also here and now, to inspire and enliven us with visions of futures worthy of our hearts and energies. In remembering the future, we prepare others and ourselves in becoming a people for justice and beloved community.

✣ ✣ ✣ ✣ ✣ ✣ ✣ ✣

Israel's prophets direct listeners to the future, not only to warn about coming destruction, but also to portray God's wondrous acts. Micah prophesied that a day is coming when God will instruct the people and bring peace among nations. His message depicts a vision of beloved community that has inspired peace activists across the centuries:

> They shall beat their swords into plowshares
>   and their spears into pruning hooks;
> nation shall not lift up sword against nation;
>   neither shall they learn war any more.
>
> (Mic. 4:3)

Micah also assures that God forgives, and that the people are not destined for a desolate future because they have sinned. Better days are ahead:

> Who is a God like you, pardoning iniquity
>   and passing over the transgression
>   of the remnant of his possession?
> He does not retain his anger forever
>   because he delights in showing steadfast love.
> He will again have compassion upon us;
>   he will tread our iniquities under foot.
> You will cast all our sins
>   into the depths of the sea.
>
> (Mic. 7:18–19)

The prophet Jeremiah reminds exiles in Babylon that God remembers the promise to bring them back to their homeland. The long period of exile has a future beyond their current distress: "For surely I know the plans I have for you, says the LORD, plans for your welfare and not for harm, to give you a future with hope" (Jer. 29:11).

Remembering the future is not a passive waiting for better times to come. God expects the exiles to live their faith even "in a strange land." Hope is there, in exile, to enliven them to life. Hear the instructive word to the exiles:

> Thus says the LORD of hosts, the God of Israel, to all the exiles whom I have sent into exile from Jerusalem to Babylon: Build houses and live in them; plant gardens and eat what they produce. Take wives and have sons and daughters; take wives for your sons, and give your daughters in marriage, that they may bear sons and daughters; multiply there, and do not decrease. But seek the welfare of the city where I have sent you into exile, and pray to the LORD on its behalf, for in its welfare you will find your welfare. (Jer. 29:4–7)

Likewise, our remembering the future defines today's discipleship. A healthier environment for our children and grandchildren involves environmental activism *now*. Limiting the ruination from mass incarceration on individuals and society involves support for criminal justice reform *now*. Reducing gun violence and its devastating impact on families and communities involves our pursuing efforts to limit access to guns *now*. Ending the demonization of enemies entails planning *now* to conduct religious education experiences that help us to live Jesus' command to "love our enemies." Reducing generational poverty means deciding to join *now* those advocacy groups and politicians who are working to repeal laws and policies that perpetuate poverty and to propose legislation that helps people overcome the factors that bind them to impoverishment.

An individual or a church cannot and should not endeavor to be involved in all these issues. Trying to engage everything would be certain to overwhelm and to negate effective involvement in anything. Choosing an issue that resonates with one's passion is a matter for *the discerning heart*. Sometimes, from circumstances we may not have anticipated, an issue chooses us. Either way, all of us are hopefully remembering the future and preparing ourselves to contribute to God's dream for the future. We have responsibility for the future.

As I remember the future, I often wonder how the coming generations, and especially children I know, will regard our prophetic witness. When they look to their "cloud of witnesses," will we be among those who inspire them to "run with perseverance the race that is set before us" (Heb. 12:1)? When they look for examples of *being prophetic*, will we come to mind? What examples will they hold of our efforts for justice and beloved community? What memories will they have of their churches engaged in *prophetic neighboring*? If they do not remember us enacting the prophetic messages of our faith's heritage, what will they conclude about us and the heritage? These questions haunt me, and they should. The questions also motivate me to remember the future. *Hope is here in remembering the future!*

In the Hebrew prophets, we have a vital heritage to inspire and tutor us. Prophetic remembering entails knowing the prophets' testimonies and enacting what they say to *us* about God's heart for compassion and justice. We are called by God to be a prophetic people whose witness is to love kindness, be involved in the struggles for justice, and walk humbly with God. A prophetic people are also called to be stewards of their history—both religious and cultural. Otherwise, the past can be manipulated and distorted to create false narratives for retaining a status quo of privilege and injustice. As a prophetic people, we have abundant opportunities to fulfill God's call through prophetic neighboring. All of us live amid suffering and injustice. All of us have the Samaritan's choice to stop and care. This we do for God's sake, for others' sake, for our own sake, and for the sake of coming generations. *Hope is here in prophetic remembering!*

Questing with Questions

1. What Scriptures are central to your prophetic remembering? Reflect on the meaning of these Scriptures for you personally and for the witness of your church.

2. What in your community's or nation's past is being forgotten, ignored, or distorted in ways that prevent us from having accurate lessons for becoming a people of beloved community? Reflect on opportunities for you and others to be stewards for a more truthful narrative.

3. Identify two or three persons who you believe are contemporary prophetic witnesses. What about their activism inspires you?

4. Recall when you have been prophetic. What motivated you to answer the call to compassion and justice? What insights and questions arise about yourself as you remember your involvement? If you do not have a memory of being prophetic, what are your thoughts about why that is the case?

5. Do you have anxieties about being prophetic? If so, what are they? If not, what has enabled you to not be anxious?

6. How would the people of your community describe your church as a neighbor? What loving acts would they name as their experience of your church?

7. As you remember the future, what prophetic concern comes to mind? What might be, or has been, your first step to engage the concern?

Chapter Five

Crossing Identity Boundaries

In every human being there runs a river of love and wisdom that can be tapped for the benefit of the world by any-
body who has the dedication, determination, and daring it
requires.

—Eknath Easwaran

[Touching] takes something from us. The power of God
passes through us to others. Through the power of touch
that heals and empowers, power is released and we become
healers to one another and to all God's creation. We do what
we have the power to do!
—Helen Bruch Pearson, *Do What You Have the Power to Do*

Boundary Clarification

Although all of us have an identity, describing it to others or even to
ourselves is difficult. How does our complexity get reduced to language? What words capture an identity that is always evolving? Still,
through life experiences with family, communities of belonging, and
commitment to ideals, an individual has a *sense of self* that professes,
"This is me."

Personal identity includes a multiplicity of cultural dimensions.
Individuals are formed and known by their race, gender, tribal and
ethnic association, language, religious affiliation, physical and mental

ableness, sexual orientation, formal education, economic status, and many other cultural groupings. Listen carefully to someone's effort to portray "This is me," and you will also hear the person's voice portraying "This is us."

Boundaries are essential to identity. Inside the boundary are the personal and cultural dimensions that characterize a person's self-understanding. The complex combination of these dimensions influences how individuals interpret their personal history, arrive at conclusions about the achievements and failings of their culture, discern purpose and meaning, determine who and what to trust, and their availability to the work of hope. An identity boundary enables a person to say, "With all the clarity, confusion, and complexity of my life, this is who I understand myself to be." Identity boundaries contribute to self-awareness.

Some dimensions of our identities are more prominent in marking the boundaries. These vary from person to person. I may name my race, faith, nurturing relationships, and vocation as the most defining boundary markers for my self-understanding and others to know me. Another person might name their citizenship, traumatic experiences, poverty, and physical disability as the most prominent markers. Clarifying the major markers can help us understand what resonates as affirming and what unsettles as threatening. If my race as a Black person is a major marker, I am attuned to interpersonal relationships and systemic forces that acknowledge and engage my racial identity. When persons say to me, "I don't see race," they may intend to convey that they "see" more than my racial identity. However, considering the significance of race to my identity, I experience their comment as *not seeing me.* Recognizing and acknowledging the significance of boundary identity markers in ourselves and others is crucial to establishing respectful and nurturing relationships that are foundational for beloved community.

This chapter stresses that being alive to life entails crossing identity boundaries—our own and those of others. Hope calls us forth to overcome alienation with love. When Jesus affirms a lawyer's answer to the question "What must I do to inherit eternal life?" (Luke 10:25), an essential part of the answer is to love "your neighbor as yourself." Jesus' answer could be restated, "And yes, with the love that pours forth from your heart, soul, strength, and mind, be compassionate with others as God desires you to be compassionate with yourself." Hope and love enliven us to ourselves and to the necessity of crossing identity boundaries to experience God's dream of beloved community.

This chapter emphasizes the importance of recognizing and understanding the multiple meanings of identity boundaries. *Boundary clarification* is important to discerning the different roles that identity boundaries play for individuals and collectives. We are wise to approach and cross our own and others' identity boundaries with awareness of their meaning. Boundaries both demarcate and protect. They clarify what most counts in self-understanding. They protect by alarming us when a crossing occurs with attitudes and actions that threaten well-being. Respecting the complexity of identity boundaries is crucial to crossing them with creative outcomes.

Crossing the identity boundaries of others and welcoming others to cross our identity boundaries are sensitive undertakings that are essential to being enlivened to life. Every organic expression of life has a boundary. Cells, plants, animals, and the collectives of tribes, cities, and nations all rely upon a larger environment for their existence. All life is interdependent. Boundaries mark where otherness and engagement begin. Convert a boundary into an impenetrable wall, and a life form is moribund. Nourishment from beyond ceases—whether the nourishment is food, water, needed resources, new ideas, or support from neighbors. Crossing identity boundaries can create and sustain the connections that are essential to vitality.

Hope compels us to be *journey bound* for identity crossings. We have the necessity and agency to do this. Our physical and spiritual growth depends on taking this journey to embrace life. The crossings are transits to seek and experience God's enlivening love in the people and places where God resides. We are created to pursue beloved community by pursuing opportunities for loving relationships. This chapter offers means to prepare for the journey and the transformations resulting from the journey.

Crossing identity boundaries, however, is not always a matter of choice. Millions of people have been forced to leave their homelands and live as *strangers in a strange land.* This is the plight of war refugees packed in camps of neighboring countries or relocated thousands of miles from a land, a people, a language, a culture, and a history that were dimensions of their identity boundary. This is also the plight of immigrants whose homeland no longer offers the food, shelter, and security needed to survive. The chapter offers insights on how even these dire realities demonstrate the work of hope in crossing identity boundaries.

Ironically, crossing identity boundaries takes us to our most fundamental identity: we are persons created by love for loving. By loving, we experience our authentic selves. We *arrive home* to ourselves and in the hearts of life. The experiences of loving relationships form us as denizens of/for beloved community.

✿✿✿✿✿✿

As mentioned, the myriad dimensions of our lives, our generational histories, and our communities constitute our identity. A person's sense of boundary will depend on those dimensions that most characterize a person's sense of self. Our bodies can signal to us and others what dimensions are lodged at our boundaries. Demeaning comments spoken to us about a family member can result in dramatic changes in our facial expressions, heart rate, and speaking volume. Receiving news that a legal right is threatened because of our gender or sexual orientation, we march in the streets and gather at legislative buildings in protest. Surprised at the outpouring of appreciation for our community service, our tears flow. Our bodies register some experiences as boundary markers. We care deeply about who we understand ourselves to be.

If we are sensitive and wise, we care deeply about other people's understandings of themselves. Our approach and crossing of their identity boundaries are done with respect and, as discussed in chapter 3, a listening heart. We pay attention to their self-identifications. For example, not all women have the same perspectives about the meaning of their gender as a boundary marker. We must listen carefully to how individuals and groups of women interpret the dimension of gender in their lives. Not all White people have the same understanding of their racial identity. For some, being White has a history of privilege that they grieve, and therefore they welcome opportunities to join persons of other races in fellowship and the struggle to over-come injustice. For others, being White has less significance than their economic and familial accomplishments. Overlooking these accom-plishments as boundary markers to then focus on their race will likely frustrate them. There are White persons who perceive themselves to be superior to other races. They understand efforts to dismantle racism as an assault on fundamental dimensions of their identity and their social standing. No dimension of identity has only a single meaning. Identity boundaries are complex and fluid. The primary way in which a person perceives oneself often changes from child-hood through adulthood. Clarifying one's own and another's identity boundary entails respecting their complexity and fluidity.

These precautions do not suggest that we must understand our own and others' boundaries fully before crossing them. Even in our first interaction with a waiter, a neighbor, a colleague, or a stranger, our very presence with them, our using or failing to use their titles (Mr., Ms., Mrs., Dr., Rev.), our words and tone of speaking, and our questions can convey our perceptions of them. We have already crossed their and our identity boundaries. Were we respectful? Do they feel seen? Do we care if they sense that we respect them? Both our momentary and long-term relationships are occasions when iden-tity boundaries are crossed. Being alert in all these situations is to rec-ognize how becoming a people for beloved community occurs in daily opportunities to demonstrate sensitivity and care.

What dimensions of your own identity are most significant to you? Write them down so that you can take the time to revisit the list and reflect on why each dimension is important to who you understand yourself to be. What do you consider to be a respectful and disrespect-ful response to each listed dimension of your identity? How have your most significant dimensions of identity changed over the years? What dimension of identity would you like to change? For example, do you want friendships with people whose religion or race or economic sta-tus is different than your own?

Being enlivened to identity boundaries can give us a more acute awareness of their bearing on emotional landscapes. We gain insight on why we welcome or resist persons who are so different than our-selves. The bases for trust or suspicion are more evident. In crossing our own boundaries, perhaps we are uncertain if encounters with others will disrupt our own sense of identity. Perhaps we are eager to release a long-held readiness to discover ourselves anew with persons and situations outside of what we have known. Clarifying how and why our identity boundaries influence our interactions with others can be a first step for a thousand more to follow. *Hope is here in boundary clarification!*

Journey Bound

Chapter 1 discusses the faith journey as a hope-inspired quest to fulfill our spirits' hunger and to give ourselves to God's dream of beloved community. The journey entails crossing identity boundaries. As with any adventure, we have expectations and plans for going from the known to the unknown. However, even with our best plans, we will have unanticipated encounters.

Journey is a major theme of Jesus' itinerant ministry. He is constantly on the move. The Gospel of Mark repeatedly uses the word "immediately" to convey the pace at which Jesus is changing locations and the pace at which transformations occur. A traditional explanation for Jesus' traveling is his need to reach many places to preach and heal. This may be true. An additional interpretation is that road travels enabled Jesus to get to people and places where he experienced God anew. Jesus experienced people who needed what he had to give *and* people whose faith inspired him.

The story of Jesus' encounter with the Syrophoenician woman is a possible example of Jesus being surprised and changed by his road experiences (Mark 7:24–30). This Gentile woman is distraught because her daughter is possessed by "an unclean spirit." She begs Jesus to heal her daughter. To this he replies, "Let the children be fed first, for it is not fair to take the children's food and throw it to the dogs." Over the centuries, such harsh words coming from Jesus have been difficult for the church to accept. Some scholars have sought to diminish the rebuke by claiming that Jesus never really questioned the woman's value as a subject of his ministry, but that he pretended disinterest in order to call forth her faith. Other scholars insist that Jesus is creating a situation of resistance so that his disciples might see the depth of this woman's faith. Some scholars suggest that "dogs" were beloved pets among the Syrophoenicians; so, the woman would not have taken offense at the comparison. Each of these interpretations attempts to rescue Jesus from an understanding of his ministry that excludes this woman.

However, another interpretation that deserves consideration is the possibility that Jesus sees this woman's request as a diversion from the mission to which God has called him. The Gospel of Matthew tells this story with an additional phrase that suggests this attitude: "I was sent only to the lost sheep of the house of Israel" (Matt. 15:24). Perhaps Jesus did not perceive that his ministry involved outreach to Gentiles. But when the woman responded, "Yes, Lord, yet even the dogs eat the crumbs that fall from their masters' table" (Matt. 15:27), a seismic shift occurred. Did Jesus hear God's call upon this woman's life as a mother—a call that challenged his interpretation of his own call? Did her persistence through a clever retort cause him to feel that she should not be denied? Did he respond to her immediately, or did he linger with her message, her tone, for a long time before answering, "Woman, great is your faith! Let it be done for you as you wish" (Matt. 15:28). In remembering this encounter, Jesus may have considered this woman to be one of his teachers. The love and hope she expressed may have expanded his ministry and helped him to be more alive to transformative encounters. Journeys that cross identity boundaries are opportunities that transform everyone—including Jesus.

Encouraging us to journey across identity boundaries is the work of hope. God's dream of justice and beloved community involves our becoming alive to the diverse expressions of life. We have agency to make the journey. Our journey might begin by initiating a conversation with a neighbor, or volunteering in a tutoring program of a school or community center, or joining an interfaith dialogue, or attending a program that focuses on dismantling racism, or discussing opportunities for community healing with a friend whose social witness you respect. Note that these suggestions involve physical engagement. While reading about social divides and crises can be informative, too often reading is the beginning and end of a person's experience. The mind ventures, and the body stays home. *Crossing identity boundaries involves relocating our bodies.*

Involving our bodies with others is the work of hope. As discussed in chapter 2, hope calls us forth from the tyranny of the familiar, fear of disappointment, and fear of suffering, to transformative experiences where God awaits us. To resist hope is to resist God's empowerment to live lives that are more aware, more engaged, and more fulfilled, through loving interactions with others.

⚜ ⚜ ⚜ ⚜ ⚜ ⚜ ⚜

Even after we have said yes to the journey, we often feel unprepared for interacting with persons whose identities are different than our own. With our intention to be respectful with others, we can still have anxieties about offending. Our questions outnumber our certainties. Do we know the etiquette of crossing the boundary of someone or of their community's identity? Are there trigger words that stoke umbrage? Are any of our questions insulting? Will mistakes be accepted as good-hearted efforts, or will they disqualify ongoing relationship? Will we feel more connected or alienated after the encounter?

The anxiety can be as intense about our own identities. We have questions that leave us uncertain about our readiness to journey. Do I know myself sufficiently for situations where matters of identity will arise? How do I avoid either having to defend my prejudiced ancestors or having to castigate them? Why am I nervous about the possible encounters? Will my demeanor manifest anxiety? Am I capable of remaining engaged if discussions turn angry? In a multireligious gathering, am I capable of being as insightful about my religion as others in the room are about their religion?

When stacked on top of one another, the questions can appear as an identity-boundary wall that reads, "Do not trespass." We need to remember that we "quest with questions." Questions alert us to matters meriting our attention. Most answers to our questions, however, are found *when we are on the journey*. We discover more about ourselves and others through our relationships. Answers sometimes come from embarrassing situations; such is the route that wisdom often takes. A greater embarrassment would be to remain sequestered behind our identity boundaries, when hope compels us to journey.

Proper intent is most significant in crossing an identity boundary. Are we motivated by the spiritual longing to overcome our alienation with others? If so, our resolve is stronger than our paralyzing anxieties. We cross with a purpose that is for our salvation (becoming whole) and contributing to beloved community. Our right intent does not prevent us from making a thousand mistakes. The mistakes may be painful, but they need not defeat us. We have the power of hope and love supporting us as we continue with the joy of the journey.

The element of intent in boundary crossings will manifest itself early or late in the ensuing relationships. Crossings driven by mere curiosity fail to convey to the other person a desire for a heart-to-heart relationship. As with nations crossing boundaries, personal purposes of domination and exploitation will ignite vehement opposition. Boundary crossings are opportunities to relate creatively with neighbors, strangers, and even enemies. When our motivations are aligned with the work of hope, we cross our own boundaries and others' identity boundaries with the vision and purpose of becoming who God has dreamed us to be with one another!

Crossing identity boundaries can be difficult and precarious. Not crossing identity boundaries is foolish and deadening—for individuals and communities. Despite the challenges, we have the necessary disciplines to journey faithfully. *Contemplative praying* with a listening heart, discerning heart, and engaging heart deepens our ability to interact with our authentic selves and with an acute sensitivity and responsiveness to others. *Prophetic remembering* keeps us in the company of prophets who embody God's message that compassion and justice must be enacted with neighbors and for coming generations. Hope is here, in these and coming disciplines, to enliven us to reconciling opportunities. We journey without excuses. We journey with hope.

❧ ❧ ❧ ❧ ❧ ❧ ❧

Millions of identity boundaries are reinforced with concrete walls, barbed wire, and guards with guns. A major dimension of these persons' reinforced identity is "prisoner." Many dimensions other than prisoner exist: family member, person of faith, falsely accused, guilty, well-educated, school dropout, skilled professional, unskilled, veteran, gang member, mentally ill, impoverished, remorseful, kindhearted, and all the other dimensions of personality found on the other side of the wall. However, the dimension of being a prisoner begins to diminish or cancel the complexity of one's sense of self. Energies given to surviving hostilities from other prisoners and guards, the soul-crushing weight of "doing time," and finding purpose in a place where society wants to punish and forget you: these reframe identity.

In his memoir, *A Question of Freedom*, Dwayne Betts writes about being a prisoner on September 11, 2001. The prison's response to the event reinforced his conclusion that prisoners' primary, if not only, identity is "incarcerated." He writes:

> I wondered what would happen if someone dropped a bomb on a prison, then I realized that no one would think to bomb a prison. We were the most expendable people in the United States and still, as soon as the first plane hit, the entire compound went on lock. We weren't allowed to make phone calls or take showers for a week. The officials didn't expect us to have family we wanted to check on. There was no sense that we would be patriotic, that our families might have been on airplanes that day or working in the Pentagon. . . . Somewhere along the line the penitentiary makes you feel more of a felon than an American.[1]

The physical walls surrounding prisons are reinforced by societal indifference. Prisons function as an identity boundary with signs that read "Nothing to see here."

Since 1976, the Rev. Janet Wolf has crossed the boundary; she has seen and been in compassionate relationship with men who live behind prison walls. Her journey has transformed her, the men involved, and those she has invited to cross the boundary. Hope has enlivened all of them to life.

In my interview with Rev. Wolf, she spoke of challenges that those in prison face to acknowledge their authentic selves while in an institution so focused on security that their prescribed daily routines deny their full humanity. Her interactions with men on death row, where freedom of movement is more restricted than in other parts of the maximum-security prison, have affirmed their gifts and capabilities. The community-building process (SALT—Schools for Alternative Learning and Transformation) she guides has enabled the men who participate to see themselves and others as more than caged outcasts.

Rev. Wolf describes SALT as an experience where everyone sits in a circle as both student and teacher. Leadership from the men in prison is essential to planning and approving courses that focus on the theologies, social institutions and systems, social inequities, cultural biases, and public indifference that perpetuate mass incarceration and its dehumanizing treatment of persons in prison.

Rev. Wolf emphasizes that participants are "invited to share the names they want to be called." Naming is crucial to the cultivation of an identity. SALT participants do not refer to persons in prison as "inmates" or "prisoners," terms they consider to be a capitulation to an unjust legal system that reduces them to their circumstances. SALT participants refer to those in prison as "insiders" or "men on death row" or "members of the SALT circle." Rev. Wolf reports, "[The SALT process] is a change for people who are in cages, who are only known by numbers or nicknames, whose voices are never valued, who are not seen or heard or really engaged as human beings. [Insiders involved in the process] will say, 'For those two hours I feel like a human being. It's the only time I feel like a human being.'"

Rev. Wolf's crossing of her and their identity boundaries has released creative life-affirming energies. She continues: "They laugh and sing, they practice amazement, they write poetry and stories, they do art, they unlearn all the [negative] things they've been told about who they are, and then let it go. . . . I never fail to be surprised and filled up by their capacity to love." The transformations are mutual.

The community-building process has involved undergraduate college students taking classes with insiders at the state's minimum-security prerelease prison, and with graduate theology students taking classes with insiders at the maximum-security prison. Insiders contribute to the development of the syllabi for courses. Faculty and students (insiders) collaborate in establishing themes and approaches for instruction. Rev. Wolf reports that professors are surprised and impressed with insiders' insightful analysis and suggestions. Insiders are awakened to their own academic skills. Collaborating on transformation projects becomes the ground on which identity crossings occur. Faculty and students (from the prison, college, and seminary) see one another as denizens in the world of ideas. Even more, they recognize the distinctive wisdom and openheartedness that emerge from their different life experiences. The impact from being companions on the journey in the classroom has forged feelings of lifelong companionship, even if the path for some is immediately to their schools, while for others their immediate path is back to their cells.

Crossing identity boundaries can be painful. Rev. Wolf has witnessed insiders, even with substantial support from prison guards and the larger community, denied parole. Men on death row active in the transformative community-building classes have been executed. Others on death row suffer the anxiety and uncertainty that arise from failures to have their cases reviewed. Sorrow travels with love. Still, the journey of hearts crossing to hearts is how we are enlivened to life. Rev. Wolf told me, "When I get ready to go to the prison, I'm usually grumpy [because of requirements to just get through the prison's security procedures]. But I always come out laughing and hopeful. . . . [The insiders] embody an alternative in the belly of the beast . . . right there on death row where the state has killed three of our circle members and seeks to kill others. They are betting everything on love." May we do likewise. *Hope is here in being journey bound!*

Strangers in a Strange Land

Crossing identity boundaries is forced on millions of people who need to escape war in their homeland. Whether the circumstances are ethnic cleansing, civil war, or invasion from a neighboring nation, deadly violence is the factor causing their flight and new identity as refugees. Survival also motivates immigrants to flee when their homeland no longer provides food, shelter, and security. Their journey across borders is also a transformation of identity. Whatever their community and professional standings in their homeland, the refugees and immigrants are now known as strangers in a strange land.

Fakhria Hussain Goksu's life in Kabul, Afghanistan, was lived with innocence and promise. Anchored by caring and hard-working parents, home provided Fakhria and her eight siblings the stability that comes from love, assurance, and joy. Still, Fakhria told me, "The most important memories of my childhood were my first year in school." She excelled in the classroom, and Fakhria's teacher frequently uplifted Fakhria's behavior and academic achievement as exemplary.

The affirmation she received at school fueled her activity at home. Fakhria says, "School was my motivation. I could not wait to go to school. In the evening I was doing homework and studying." Growth through formal education excited her. Along with her identity as a daughter and sister was the passion for being a student.

She completed first grade. Although eager to continue her education, deadly violence overtook normal life in Kabul. Various groups fought to control the government, and criminal gangs took advantage of the disorder with abductions and robbery. Anxiety pervaded among Kabul's citizens. Gunshots were heard throughout the city. The lethal environment ended Fakhria's ability to attend school. No longer in school, Fakhria and her siblings were taught carpet weaving by their parents, just to keep them safe at home.

The family's fears took a devastating turn when Fakhria's youngest brother was shot in the back and brought unconscious by neighbors to the family. After he was taken to the hospital, doctors concluded that a bullet could not be safely removed because it was too close to his spinal column. He survived, but the injury would lead to years of chronic health challenges.

Endeavoring to find a safe place to live, the family relocated several times in Afghanistan. But the violence in Kabul spread throughout the country. Leaving Afghanistan for neighboring Pakistan emerged as the best option for their safety. The journey to Pakistan, however, was precarious. After a three-hour walk with extended family members, they arrived at a house to rest and retreat from the dangers that surrounded them. Women and children went to the basement. Men waited outside as guards. This would be the last time that Fakhria would see her father alive. A bomb exploded outside; her father and the other guardians were killed. The bomb also shattered her experience of being part of a whole family. His death was traumatic for her, and her profound grief as a seven-year-old would linger into her adult years.

The realities of being a refugee in Pakistan deepened her grief. In addition to the death of her father, Fakhria experienced the end of her identity as a promising student. In Pakistan, she could not attend school, because the family needed her carpet-making labor for income. Every family member, including her four-year old sister, had to contribute to the family's carpet-making enterprise. Six days a week they worked twelve hours a day, with a one-hour break. To afford a place to live, they were always in a house with other families. The ten members of her family lived and worked in only one room. Describing her routine and feelings, she says:

> We didn't go outside. I learned most from television. Emotionally, there were times that I did not really feel I was alive. I kind of felt I was an object moving my hands working, eating, sleeping. . . . I had kind of lost sensation. As a child, after age seven, I didn't get to play, have friends, go to school. It almost seems that my childhood ended at age seven.

Her means of coping with the drudgery was to daydream and to pursue joyful dreams in sleep. She recalls:

> One of my pleasures was [when] I tried to go to bed early. I wanted to see things that I couldn't experience in life. I wanted to see them in my dreams—going to school, playing, seeing my friends, my relatives. . . . I was planning to see those things in my dreams. My first-grade teacher [back in Afghanistan] became the imagined support for my life. That kept me motivated. I always dreamed about school. And I'd see my teacher in my dreams.

Fakhria's living conditions were distressing; but she also had enlivening forces of love to sustain her hopefulness. Her mother was an inspiring example of strength and determination, despite being ill and having the stress of responsibility for the family. Fakhria's older brothers took roles that assisted their mother in providing the essentials for the family to survive. Fakhria recalls that the family functioned as a "team" and with coherence that gave her assurance. The dimension of caring family in her identity was crucial to her physical and emotional survival.

Fakhria's Muslim faith was an enlivening force in these distressing years. She answered the Muslim tradition of being called to prayer five times a day. Her daily prayer times increased during Ramadan.

The monthlong Ramadan fast of not eating and drinking during the day was "exciting" and rejuvenating. Fakhria describes the meaning of her religious practices as nourishment on the journey:

> Faith was important to my family, and it helped us . . . during the difficult time. Also, it was a break. For me, personally, when I prayed it was just a nice, peaceful time for myself. I felt strong. I felt supported. I felt relief while in a strange country where we did not have family and friends. We did not know our neighbors, but we stayed connected with Allah. We felt protected and safe.

After living in Pakistan for ten years, some members of Fakhria's family were finally accepted as refugees in the United States. The move required the family to divide, since children over eighteen (except for the health-challenged brother) could not come to the United States. Her dreaming shifted from reminiscing about the past to anticipating her future. She would no longer have to work, and she could begin to fulfill her desire to return to school. Three months before coming to the United States, the family members who had been accepted as refugees took English classes to learn such basics as writing their names and addresses, and how to introduce themselves.

The transition to living in the United States was difficult. Her mother had never worked outside the home and needed employment. Her ill brother needed to secure work. Fakhria was seventeen with no formal education since the first grade in Kabul, and she had minimal English skills. She enrolled in a public high school and took English as a Second Language classes. Despite the age difference with other first-year high-school students, she was excited to be a student and "studied nonstop because I was so happy and grateful to be given a second chance to be in school." Fakhria also attended a "Saturday school" program that developed her academic skills.

Being older than her peers in the same high-school grade level led to hurtful teasing. She was also bullied because she was Muslim and Hussain was her last name. Students would taunt her by asking, "How are you related to Saddam Hussein?" and "Are you also a terrorist?" Despite the bullying, working after school and weekends, and sleeping only four to five hours a day, Fakhria pursued her dream to excel in school. She says: "Those [negative] things did not stop me because I was focused on learning. I was motivated by the positive things." Fakhria had "positive" experiences: high-school teachers who cared for her academic and emotional needs, Saturday school tutors, a mentor who took a personal interest in her thriving, and others who responded to her requests for assistance.

Fakhria graduated from high school at age twenty-one and received a scholarship to Berry College. This was another difficult transition for her. College classes were more demanding than her high-school education. She worked twenty hours a week to secure needed finances. The unexpected death of her brother, who drowned in a swimming pool, was the overwhelming shock that left her feeling bereft of hope. Fakhria felt like "giving up" and that her dream "was over." The loss of her brother seemed unbearable. The caring response of Berry professors and students enabled her to return to school and resume her dream. At twenty-five years of age, after a life of enormous challenges, Fakhria graduated from Berry College.

Fakhria has dedicated her life to the creative formation of children and to healing persons who have experienced trauma. She has worked and volunteered as a teacher, social worker, and case manager for persons coping with trauma and stress. Fakhria's journeys to strange lands prepared her for the work of beloved community in her new homeland.

⚜ ⚜ ⚜ ⚜ ⚜ ⚜ ⚜

Refugees and immigrants cross identity boundaries because of the necessity to survive. Their journeys occur because of dire circumstances beyond their control. A thousand uncertainties await. However, the immediate question is, Will we be welcomed, or forced to return, or taken to another country's borders to pursue entry? They are strangers in strange lands; their greatest need is hospitality.

The Bible stresses hospitality to strangers in a strange land as an act of faith that honors what God requires of us. God instructs Moses to tell the Israelites: "You shall not oppress a resident alien; you know the heart of an alien, for you were aliens in the land of Egypt" (Exod. 23:9). God gives a law and says they can identify with the "heart" of a foreigner because they (the Israelites) were foreigners in a strange land. God calls them to recognize the foreigner's identity in their own experience. Crossing identity boundaries inspires empathy born from seeing myself in another.

God repeats the instruction to "not oppress" resident aliens and expands the requirement to "love" the aliens: "When an alien resides with you in your land, you shall not oppress the alien. The alien who resides with you shall be to you as the native-born among you; you shall love the alien as yourself, for you were aliens in the land of Egypt: I am the LORD your God" (Lev. 19:33–34). The prophet Jerimiah *remembers* the God-given law and says: "Act with justice and righteousness and deliver from the hand of the oppressor anyone who has been robbed. And do no wrong or violence to the alien" (Jer. 22:3). Acting with "righteousness" and "doing no wrong" involve attending to the needs of those who suffer from oppressive circumstances. Jesus' parable about the Samaritan who provided for the long-term care of a beaten and incapacitated stranger instructs us on our responsibility across identity boundaries (Luke 10:25–37).

Extending hospitality to strangers involves crossing identity boundaries. Differences in language, culture, and background often make communication awkward. Refugees and immigrants fleeing for survival have profound identity differences from their hosts. Despite such complexity and confusion, crossing identity boundaries occurs. Language differences are overcome with translators and gestures of welcome. A smile is a universal expression that invites connection. Food, shelter, clothing, and directions are offerings that signal compassion, even when cultural and background differences are acute. These gestures and offerings disclose hearts.

When we are hosts in hospitality, *contemplative praying* prepares us for crossing identity boundaries with strangers. Having experienced God's presence in prayer, we carry that awareness into hosting. We relax our anxieties about being insufficient. We trust hope's enlivening work. With a "listening heart," "discerning heart," and "engaging heart," we cross identity thresholds to experience the heart of another. Our hearts rejoice in the experience of compassionate fellowship. When efforts prove disappointing, we lament and work to overcome whatever separates us from heart-to-heart relationships.

When hosts welcome refugee and immigrant guests to a place and time of fellowship, the crossings of identity boundaries are mutual. Hosts engage guests' journeys with sensitivity to guests' desire to tell their stories and to choose silence about realities too painful to speak. Guests engage hosts' commitment and journeys to offer hospitality with their strenuous efforts and despite limited resources. Crossing another's identity boundary is a mutual enlivening of hearts. Alienation is diminished. Hosts and guests cross together into experiences of beloved community.

✣✣✣✣✣✣✣

I facilitated the post-pilgrimage discussion of teenagers who had visited the Dexter Avenue King Memorial Baptist Church in Montgomery, Alabama, where Martin Luther King Jr. had been the pastor. They mentioned the docent's report on her experience with a previous group of young students. After speaking about the sacrifices made by civil rights activists that made current rights and freedoms possible, she asked the youth, "For what are you willing to die?" A fourth-grader responded, "Strangers." When I heard this account, chills ran through my body—and the chills return every time I recall the response. What led this fourth grader to declare this commitment to strangers? Who taught him? Was this emphasized in his religious education? How many adults would give the same answer?

Children are repeatedly told to avoid relationships with strangers. Child abductions are lasting nightmares for families and communities. The mistrust of strangers, however, is not restricted to children. Adults are leery of strangers in their neighborhoods. Villagers look upon "outsiders" with suspicion. National leaders and citizens will characterize refugees and immigrants as invaders. Theologian William May says, "It is well to remember that the word for stranger and the word for enemy in many languages is one and the same term."[2] Perhaps language announces a reaction embedded in our DNA: strangers merit our fear and hostility.

The suspicion and fear of strangers function as a "Do not trespass!" barrier to identity boundary crossings. Even when we are aware of the flight and plight of refugees and immigrants, we may be influenced by narratives about their being a threat to our safety, economy, educational and healthcare institutions, and identity. These are our challenges. Keeping a distance from strangers may seem to serve our security, when it actually obstructs personal growth and beloved community.

Fakhria's story is one of escaping war, crushed dreams, traumatic family deaths, existing in a strange land, exhausting work, an uncertain future, and despair. Her story also includes Afghanis who helped the family to escape, Pakistanis who received and assisted the family, resettlement agencies that made coming to the United States possible, local refugee agencies that welcomed and provided needed housing and employment opportunities, schools that provided programs to restart her education, teachers and mentors who took a personal interest in her, and counselors who guided her to address her trauma. Fakhria was a stranger in strange lands who experienced the caring hearts of strangers. Her identity boundary had crossing after crossing as she also crossed beyond the identity boundaries of those who helped her. These boundary crossing journeys enlivened Fakhria to life, and they enlivened those who gave her hospitality in its many forms. *Hope is here enlivening strangers in (and the people of) strange lands!*

Arriving Home

Journey is usually understood as leaving home for distant destinations. A faith journey may take us to distant places, or a local prison, or a refugee agency, or a homeless shelter, or a hospital, or a neighbor we have never met, or a conversation with a stranger. In these places, hope empowers us to cross identity boundaries and to be enlivened to life anew. In crossing identity boundaries, the heart is subject to being experienced as a host, guest, stranger, enemy, and/or friend. When we arrive in these places of relationship, we arrive where God has long awaited us. We arrive home!

The journey is more than a means to destinations. The journey itself is a destination. In crossing identity boundaries, we meet God anew on the journey. Here we perceive the world and ourselves with greater depth. Our true selves bathe in the assurance of God's sustaining presence where we are nurtured, energized, and rested. In other words, as people of faith, we are home.

Jesus describes the love that is ultimately meaningful in God's realm. Care for the body exemplifies the focus and work of love. Jesus spoke of the hungry body being fed, the thirsty body being given drink, the strange body being welcomed, the naked body being clothed, the sick body receiving care, and the imprisoned body being visited (Matt. 25:31–46). Body conditions are holy matters. To deny loving care to persons and their body conditions is to deny love to God. The body, as a recipient and giver of loving care, is of holy and ultimate significance.

Care for others' bodies involves addressing the dimensions of their identity (hunger, thirst, alienation, nakedness, illness, imprisonment) that inflict suffering and possibly distort their sense of self. Providing food and drink to those in need is good. However, these persons are more than empty stomachs or an exhausted workforce. Offering safe camps to refugees is good. However, they are more than fleeing strangers. Giving clothes to naked people is good. However, their nakedness is more than a condition that needs covering. Caring for the sick is good. However, they are more than whatever confines them to a bed. Visiting prisoners is good. However, they are more than the factors (whether just or unjust) resulting in their incarceration. Loving care involves perceiving and honoring *the person* and not just their conditions. When we see people only as their conditions, we shrink their identity and our hearts. More than to a body in need, hope enlivens us to *the person* with needs.

Some Bible covenants extend beyond the immediate generation with which a covenant was initiated. Establishing a covenant with Abraham, God says, "I will establish my covenant between me and you and your offspring after you throughout their generations, for an everlasting covenant, to be God to you and to your offspring after you" (Gen. 17:7). We are blessed to inherit covenants that define our relationships. Long ago, our faith ancestors knew that any hope for God's dream of beloved community depended on crossing identity boundaries. Kindness to strangers is one of the most difficult and most necessary boundary crossings. Even when current cultural mores discourage interacting with strangers, we have inherited a covenantal commitment to care and extend hospitality to them. At times, our hearts know and respond to this commitment before our minds decide.

An illustration of this occurred in the experience of my student who signed up for an overseas summer internship. He confessed that although the goals of the internship focused on immersion in another country to broaden perspectives on cultural diversity, he primarily anticipated enjoying the country's beaches and party life as advertised on television commercials. He would do the internship's required work, but his real motivation was to relax and have fun.

One day while shopping during the internship, he heard a commotion across the street. He was shocked to see a mob of people beating a man. Without hesitation he ran across the street and threw his body over the beaten man. The mob insisted that he leave or he would receive the same treatment. He asked why they were trying to kill this man, and they shouted back their accusations that the man had injured a woman they knew. The student still refused to budge from protecting the man and held his ground until the police came to rescue the man and him.

When I debriefed the student about his internship experiences, I asked why he intervened in this situation. He was in a strange land among a people of a different race and culture. He had no history with the man under attack, the injured woman, or those in the mob. The student replied, "I don't know why I did what I did. I saw someone's life at stake, and something in me had to respond. I've never done anything like this before, but I had to do it." The bond that this student had with the assaulted man did not arise from previous contact with him. Together they were in a place and time where the covenantal obligation to care for strangers engulfed the student's heart. His willingness to sacrifice his own body was not an impulsive act of folly, but an impulsive response to a covenant obligation to care for strangers that his body knew he had inherited. While even in a strange land, he arrived home.

⚜ ⚜ ⚜ ⚜ ⚜ ⚜ ⚜

Jesus journeys with twelve friends whom he asked to join him in bearing witness to God's dream of compassion and justice flourishing in hearts and throughout the land. The twelve are usually understood to be his disciples, whose purpose is to perpetuate the significance of Jesus and his witness beyond all their lifetimes. In addition to this role, the twelve may be the community Jesus *needed* for the coming known and unknown realities of his ministry. His community of friends would be companions who lessened his loneliness, affirmed and challenged his convictions, stimulated his insights, retold their experiences with humor and questions, and expressed compassion for him and one another. Friendship is crucial to the work of love and hope—for individuals and for beloved community.

Friendships come with a thousand variations. Friends with whom you have common life experiences, and friends whose life experiences are dramatically different than yours. Friends with whom you resonate on personal and social matters, and friends with whom you have vehement debates about everything. Friends who speak their hearts to you, but seldom inquire about your heart. Friends who ask about your life, while withholding what stirs within theirs. Friends with whom you have regular times of connection, and friends with infrequent contact. Friends who seem to reach out only when they are in a crisis, and friends who communicate even when they have nothing in particular to talk about.

With all their complexity and complications, friendships expand our hearts and nurture us on our journeys. They are necessary in our formation as a people for beloved community. Friendships tutor us in crossing identity boundaries. We learn how availability, words, silence, tears, and laughter are received in contributing to a relationship. We discern what we are ready to offer of ourselves as a friend crosses our boundary. Our hearts are guests and hosts. Hospitality, in its varied forms for these varied relationships, characterizes the boundary crossings of friendships. Our task is to understand how hope enlivens us to hospitality.

The friendship journey relies upon trust. Opening your heart to someone exposes cherished and embarrassing aspects of identity. A friend is expected to respect the vulnerability that occurs from being openhearted. Dreams and secrets are held in confidence. Promises are fulfilled. Loving-kindness characterizes the relationship. A reliable friend engenders intimacy, healing, growth, concern, sacrifice, and joy. Friends are cherished companions for the journey's many seasons.

Consequently, when trust is squandered by a friend, deep feelings of disappointment and violation erupt. Not only is the friendship jeopardized, but the journey also suffers painful disruption. With the absence of the beloved with whom I entrusted my heart, what new vulnerabilities await? How did I misread our friendship? Why risk exposing my heart again?

The psalmist depicts the severe attack upon the heart caused by betrayed friendship. The emotional response to the injury exceeds anger and rushes to vengeance:

> It is not enemies who taunt me—
>> I could bear that;
> it is not adversaries who deal insolently with me—
>> I could hide from them.
> But it is you, my equal,
>> my companion, my familiar friend,
> with whom I kept pleasant company;
>> we walked in the house of God with the throng.
> Let death come upon them;
>> let them go down alive to Sheol,
>> for evil is in their homes and in their hearts.
>> (Ps. 55:12–15)

As we oppose the remedy spoken by the injured psalmist, we need to acknowledge the devastating impact of betrayals. Crossing an identity boundary and becoming a friend are sacred initiatives with immense consequences.

In Jesus' circle of friends, Judas's betrayal resulted in Jesus' crucifixion, Peter denied knowing Jesus after his arrest; others scattered in fear for their lives. I imagine that Jesus had been mindful of their frailties and the likelihood of abandonment. Still, these are the friends with whom Jesus desired to be in table fellowship in his final hours. Sometimes the enlivening power of friendship survives disheartening ordeals and even death.

Cultivating friendships is an initiative we must take in becoming people for beloved community. We need friends for the journey of being enlivened to life. In God's calling for us to be companions on the journey, we discover so much about the complexity, perils, and joy of crossing identity boundaries.

What stands out about your list of friends? What dimensions of identity (e.g., race, gender, ethnicity, economic status, sexual orientation, religion, generation, education, vocation, etc.) are similar among your friends, and what dimensions are diverse? Where do you locate yourself among the noted similarities and diversity? How do you interpret the various relationships? Which are close? Which are more casual? What pleases you about your friendships? In terms of your personal growth, what types of relationships are absent in your circle of friends?

Regarding friendship, in the United States, as well as many countries in the world, people with intellectual disabilities (i.e., Down syndrome and other neurodevelopmental disorders) have often suffered isolation from family and societal interactions. Their lives have been consigned to institutions where professional staff and visiting family were their main relationships. I have heard parents of children with intellectual disabilities complain that their children are denied participation in the full life of their churches and synagogues. The failure of congregations to reenvision their religious practices to include intellectually disabled persons negates opportunities for members to experience their houses of worship as boundary-crossing bridges for enlivening new friendships.

L'Arche is a creative movement to provide boundary crossings. Operating on six continents, L'Arche (meaning "The Ark" in French) has established neighborhood homes and work opportunities for persons with intellectual disabilities. Friendships occur between persons with intellectual disabilities (called "core members" in the homes) and persons without intellectual disabilities (assistants in the homes, family members, and supporters from the larger community). They eat, play, work, travel, rest, and worship together. Some core members are very communicative, while others are mostly silent. Some are insightful in their interactions with the world, while others seem confused in their efforts to interpret their world. Some are quite mobile, while others have such severe physical disabilities that they depend on assistants for their most basic body needs. Some are caring and gracious, while others are self-absorbed and demanding. Of course, each core member can be a mixture of these personality traits and more. Relationships with these companions can be a joy and can be extremely difficult.

With this great variety of characteristics and relationships, the consistent testimony of those who assist core members is that their lives are transformed and enriched by their relationships with core members. Tim Kearney, who has worked in L'Arche since 1982, writes about his relationships with two core members, Danny and Edith. His reflection on his intimate relationship with them speaks the conviction of thousands affiliated with L'Arche:

> L'Arche's spirituality is based on the particular insight that God is hidden in the most vulnerable and broken people in our community and that [God] is also hidden in a special way in those parts of my own being that are vulnerable and weak. . . .
>
> I have discovered through my friendship with Edith and Danny and others, the paradox that they have been a source of healing for me through their unconditional acceptance of me as I am and through their simple trust in me. They have helped me to see that the healing process in L'Arche is a mutual and reciprocal one. It is to the extent that we suffer together, and share the hurts, that we also grow together.[3]

Friendships with intellectually disabled persons are not just about addressing their needs. Such friendships enliven all involved to the transformative power of presence. Relationships where social status, intellectual dueling, common backgrounds, and personal failures are not the currency for friendships will then enable deeper matters to recast friendship. Prayerful listening, to others and to one's own true self's guidance, bonds friendships. Releasing efforts to hide vulnerabilities makes the heart more available to another. Discovering ways to express understanding and care beyond relying on words brings forth new possibilities for communicating. The most authentic bases for friendship replace extraneous desires to impress another.

⚜ ⚜ ⚜ ⚜ ⚜ ⚜

Noting boundary crossings with friends, neighbors, prisoners, refugees, strangers, and intellectually disabled persons is *not* about making a comprehensive checklist for upcoming identity crossings. First, a comprehensive checklist is neither possible nor the point. We continually face new expressions of identity that announce their place in community. For example, cultural controversies have emerged over acknowledging persons who identify as transgender. Arguments erupt about legal gender status, use of restrooms, participation in sports, acceptance in religious congregations, hiring discrimination, appropriate pronouns, and other related issues. In addition to the transgender example, "new expressions of identity" occur in matters of race, ethnicity, nationality, disability, religion, and social class. A draft version for a comprehensive identity checklist would be outdated before the ink dried.

More important, *crossing identity boundaries is about how we are transformed,* and not just about increasing the number of boundaries crossed. Boundary clarification leads to asking, How are we more aware and responsive to another's, and our own, sense of self? How are we sensitive to the social circumstances (e.g., poverty, discrimination, incarceration) that influence identity? How might we be in solidarity with others to overcome systemic forces that oppress persons we now know? What are we understanding about ourselves in these crossings? What are matters of etiquette and hospitality in boundary crossings? How do we perceive God's presence on both sides of a boundary? If these journey questions are ignored whenever we cross an identity boundary, we could cross a thousand boundaries with no greater wisdom and heart transformation. These questions guide us home with expanded hearts.

This chapter's focus on hope's enlivening work through relationships highlights the necessity to be *journey bound*. We travel to people and their contexts to cross their identity boundaries and to invite them to cross our boundaries. Ultimately, cultivating understanding and trust involve being in physical relationship. So much of what we communicate about ourselves is nonverbal, and greater understanding from speech occurs in face-to-face settings. The journey is an adventure to overcome the alienation of being apart by opening our hearts to one another.

Beloved community struggles to exist when fear of strangers is stronger than extending hospitality. Resistance to receiving refugees and immigrants (*strangers in a strange land*) is a major manifestation of this fear. We are wise to remember prophetically our faith ancestors, who counsel us to embrace the plight of strangers as hospitality opportunities. Strangers bring not only their needs, but also their inspiring example of persevering with hope. Crossing identity boundaries is hope's way of overcoming alienation and despair in strangers and hosts. Our seeking hearts yearn to reside in hospitality. *Hope is here to enliven us in arriving home!*

Because crossing identity boundaries is so elemental to beloved community, Howard Thurman concludes that every effort must be made to eliminate any personal attitude or cultural barrier that prevents people from being in caring relationship. The love ethic depends on such meetings. Thurman writes:

> The experience of love is either a necessity or a luxury. If it be a luxury, it is expendable; if it be a necessity, then to deny it is to perish. So simple is the reality, and so terrifying. Ultimately there is only one place of refuge on this planet for any [person]—that is in another [person's] heart. To love is to make of one's heart a swinging door.[4]

Hope enlivens us, as hosts and guests, to the hospitality invitation of the "swinging door." The journey through the swinging door leads to a place where we are formed for beloved community. *Hope is here in crossing identity boundaries!*

Questing with Questions

1. Among the questions posed in this chapter, identify one or two that are especially compelling for your ongoing reflection. What makes the question(s) compelling?
2. What do you want others to know about your sense of self? What about your sense of self do you withhold from persons?
3. How does your church facilitate members crossing identity boundaries? What are some outcomes from these experiences?

4. Think of an experience when you received hospitality as a stranger. What occurred? What feelings and ongoing thoughts do you have about the experience?

5. Where are places of hospitality in your community? What do you perceive as their significance to your community?

6. How do you nurture your friendships? How satisfied are you with your answer?

7. Reflect on a time when you felt that being with friends or strangers was a sacred experience. What occurred that brought forth this sacred feeling?

Chapter Six

Transforming Conflict

The crossroads we encounter as we seek to be faithful servants are often excruciating because we know how much is at stake, how vital the mission is, that it really matters to get it right not for our own sake but for the children and the cause we seek to serve.

—Marian Wright Edelman,
"Prophetic Service and Global Change"

Resentment is like drinking poison and then hoping it will kill your enemy.

—Nelson Mandela

Befriending Conflict

Conflict has a bad reputation. We lament the broken relationships within our families and friendships, and conflict is usually named as the culprit. We see conflict active where we work, and anxiety increases as we foresee its impact on our camaraderie and our livelihood. The very center that holds together congregations, communities, and countries seems ruptured by conflict. The devastating outcomes are evidence for conflict's bad reputation.

However, like many other misplaced accusations, conflict gets blamed for problems caused by other factors. Conflict may result from a broken promise in a friendship. A congregation may be in turmoil over issues of sexual orientation and gender identity. Communities are battlegrounds for protesters and counterprotesters over issues of racial discrimination, hospitality to immigrants, gun control, and public-education curricula. Nations dispute with neighboring countries the borders that define ownership of natural resources. In all these situations, conflict *results* from betrayals, contrasting beliefs, injustice, fear, prejudice, greed, or distrust. Often, blaming conflict as the problem becomes a means to avoid addressing what has caused the conflict. When we engage the causes of conflicts, and not just the manifestations of conflicts, we are more likely to heal ancient and current wounds.

God's peace (shalom) is about the flourishing of compassion and justice. God's peace is not defined by the absence of conflict. Throughout the Hebrew Scriptures, God calls prophets to oppose the cultural practices and ruling authorities whose indifference and greed cause people to suffer. Jesus' ministry challenges religious leaders' interpretations of faith practices (such as keeping the Sabbath) and forbidden intimacy with the "unclean" and "sinners." The reaction from religious authorities and Rome's collaborators results in his public execution. The path to beloved community can disrupt and bring forth fierce opposition. Conflict is not only a means to peace; conflict is often a prerequisite for peace.

This chapter focuses on the importance of *befriending conflict* to gain deeper insight into its causes and its complexities, and how to engage it creatively. If we try to keep our distance from conflict and ascribe only detrimental outcomes to it, we fail to appreciate that conflict provides opportunities for understanding, healing, and new beginnings of trust and collaboration for a creative future. In befriending conflict, we open our minds and hearts to transformative insights about ourselves, about our relationships, and about conflict.

Conflicts have multiple outcomes—some deadly, others life giving. *Befriending transformation* enables us to pursue outcomes that align with justice and beloved community. When we are available to transformative opportunities in conflict, and not fixated on our anxiety and eagerness to be done with conflict, we perceive opportunities for our spiritual practices and training to transform volatile situations into reconciling ones. This chapter discusses how the spiritual practices of the previous chapters foster creative outcomes for transforming conflict.

Transforming conflict also involves transforming organizations and systems that perpetuate suffering and injustice. Social unrest is exacerbated and human relationships are strained by institutions that fail to assure necessities for living, opportunities for growth, and justice. Initiating conflict can be a means to address oppressive and suffocating social realities. For example, the civil rights movement organized protest marches, sit-ins, and boycotts to transform the systemic violence of discrimination in access to housing and employment, voting rights, police brutality, and urban planning projects that destroyed Black communities. Environmental activists disrupt oil pipeline construction, block trucks that dump chemical waste near residences and in oceans, and file lawsuits against construction that encroaches on endangered species. *Initiating conflict can be a transformational activity* for getting into what congressman and civil rights activist John Lewis called "good trouble."

Arriving at beloved community entails *befriending forgiveness.* Ancient and recent injuries cause alienation and hatred. This alienation foments resentment and distrust. The wounds that ancestors and neighbors experienced from conflict remain open. They fester. Hatred emerges as a salve for the wounds and pain. Revenge lurks as a pain-relieving option. Hatred begets hatred. Violence begets violence. The never-ending cycles require a dramatic intervention that liberates hearts to begin the healing process. Forgiveness is the necessary and powerful intervention that transforms the death spiral of conflicts into reconciling opportunities.

The chapter ends with the transformative role of *love* in conflict. Chapter 1 noted that hope and love are always together as enlivening forces of God that empower and guide us toward beloved community. Whatever is the challenge for hope is the challenge for love. Together, *they transform conflict by transforming us.* We are free to reject hope or to give ourselves to the enlivening work of hope and love. The choice is not easy. The work of hope and love makes demands upon us that transform habits, relationships, and commitment. With all the complex situations of life and myriad considerations in discernment, hope and love guide us to face a simple yet life-changing decision: *sacrifice.*

⚜ ⚜ ⚜ ⚜ ⚜ ⚜ ⚜

We have benchmarks to gauge our relationship with conflict. When you reflect on various settings where conflict occurs—job, church, extended family, public meetings, one-on-one relationships—where are you most willing to actively engage with conflict? What subjects— sexuality, race relations, politics, religious convictions, money—do you resist discussing if feelings in the room are intense? How different is your emotional reaction when you are the focus of a conflict and not just a discussant about a conflict? What identity groups, different from your identity, do you avoid for fear of conflict? Reflecting on your answers can bring forth insights on the circumstances that influence your readiness to befriend conflict.

These questions are *not* a guise to infer you should be at ease with conflict in all the settings, with all the subjects, and with all the identities. With wisdom we choose when and where to devote our emotional energies to settings with conflict. The questions aid our discerning hearts to grasp why we accept or reject life's invitations into conflict situations. We are better able to confront ourselves in asking, How do my reticence and refusal to be involved with certain contexts of conflict impact my commitment to justice and beloved community? How is my true self becoming prepared to transform conflict to advance justice and the coming of beloved community? Befriending conflict involves acknowledging and releasing anxieties that obstruct our being enlivened to life.

Fear of conflict appears in a variety of dysfunctional behaviors. The impact on groups or organizations can be especially consequential when the dysfunctional behavior is in leadership. For example, leaders who are conflict adverse will make quick decisions or will continually defer a controversial matter, in order to avoid anticipated conflict. Domineering leaders may present themselves as bold visionaries, but their fear of conflict often propels their bluster in declaring a decision. Leaders and group members weary of heated discussions will insist that a vote be taken so that attention can turn to more pleasant business. All these behaviors fail to address the causes of conflict and leave intense feelings unaddressed.

The proverbial comment that "we have not acknowledged the elephant in the room" refers to relevant and major issues that are ignored. The elephant is interpreted to be an obvious and disruptive beast. Failure to engage the elephant does not result in positive outcomes. If some group members want to talk about the elephant, but the meeting concludes without a discussion, resentments fester. Persons may physically remain throughout the meeting while their commitment has already left the room. Befriending conflict may not result in a group arriving at consensus; however, persons are more likely to appreciate a process and participate in the resulting decisions when they and their concerns are heard and respected.

The effort to ignore or evade conflict is futile and counterproductive. Whether daily or episodic, anticipated or surprising, small scale or systemic, dormant or fever pitched, respectful or deadly, conflict will always be with us. We are wise to befriend it. Soon or late, ignored conflict turns on us with ferocity.

The commitment to befriend conflict is *not* a mandate to become involved in the conflicts of all the places where we live, move, and have our being. No one has the time or energy to be embroiled in that quantity of conflicts. As I stated about *invitations* in chapter 2, "trying to be everywhere diminishes genuine involvement anywhere." We must discern where to devote ourselves to taking a stand amid the myriad opportunities to enter the fray.

Befriending conflict, as with the previously discussed spiritual practices, involves our bodies being present. The listening/discerning/engaging heart, being prophetic, and crossing identity boundaries place our bodies in caring relationships. The work of hope and love entails physical proximity—not only a face-to-face proximity, but also an ability to embrace. Therefore, befriending conflict goes far beyond being familiar with theories and methods about transforming conflict. An intimate relationship with conflict is always emotional. As in a friendship, we befriend conflict by being physically close to it, understanding its complex character through relationship, and offering our hearts.

Our bodies register our discomfort with conflict. A racing heart, a quivering voice, a shaking hand, and flowing tears are signs of feelings behind the words spoken and unspoken. Some people choose to forgo being involved in conflict situations that trigger these reactions. Others decide that their involvement is more consequential than their discomfort; so they persist in expressing themselves, even if they are embarrassed by their physical signs of being nervous. Situations of conflict are emotional crucibles that reveal us to ourselves. *How we respond to the revelation can be as important as the revelation.*

Years ago, I decided to become certified as a conflict mediator. The training and certification would prepare me to mediate cases referred from governmental courts, community organizations, and individuals in dispute. My motivation was not primarily about becoming a mediator; I most wanted to be more engaged in situations of conflict. With considerable ease, I had organized protest marches, occupied a government office, and confronted public officials on justice issues. Still, in professional and community gatherings I failed to speak, even though I wanted to contribute to debated matters. I chose mediation training to liberate myself from feeling shackled by discomfort in certain situations. Importantly, I also knew that my future opportunities to contribute to creative institutional and community outcomes would require my full availability to participate in conflict.

In mediating my first cases, I was aware of how my body was tense and nervous about showing anxiety. Before long, I was mediating amid grievous narratives, fierce arguments, and unsettling emotions with a personal sense of being undisturbed by the conflicts. It was as surprising as it was desired. *I was more involved with the hearts and matters in conflict than with my anxiety about conflict.* Pursuing a healing way forward focused my energies. My composure in these situations signaled that I was befriending conflict. I continued to befriend conflict not only as a mediator, but also when involved as the subject of a conflict.

Fundamentally, befriending conflict is to be alive to more realities of life. Conflict is a given on our journey. We may have personal times of extended tranquility. Even then, conflict occurs in the vicinity or just beyond the horizon. We know of conflicts that need transformation in order for compassion to replace injury; and there are conflicts that beckon us to join the struggle for justice. For ill or good, conflict always awaits us, and conflict awaits befriending.

When we devote our energies to evading conflict, our true selves languish in anxiety and fear. We then miss the lessons that conflict teaches us about our capacities, our transformative relationships, and the malleability of systems. Fortunately, when we embrace conflict, we embrace an option that liberates our true selves and guides us toward beloved community. *Hope is here in befriending conflict!*

Befriending Transformation

As we face opportunities to become new, we may feel ambiguous about opportunities that both call us from comfort zones and hold the promise of living "a big life." Transformation can both unsettle and enliven. When our own transformation involves befriending conflict, we often look for other options. However, no other viable option exists. Conflict awaits on the path for personal transformation and establishing beloved community. Befriending a future worth anticipating involves befriending transformation.

This chapter's emphasis on transforming conflict is *not* instruction on the professional field of "conflict transformation"—a field that has distinctive approaches to conflict. My emphasis aligns with the "professional field" in these ways: identifying the deeper causes of conflict, engaging creative outcomes from conflict, and interpreting the significance of systemic realities to conflicts. In addition, my focus is on how our spiritual practices can form us for transformation. As we give ourselves to enacting spiritual practices that help us to transform conflict, we are transformed. We can answer faithfully God's call to heal alienated relationships and unjust systems.

The spiritual practice of *contemplative listening*, as an expression of contemplative praying, connects us with the wisdom of our authentic selves. When I am centered with my authentic self, false narratives about my needs and capacity are dismissed or rewritten. In a conflict, I do not need to win or be liked; but I do need for the concerns of my heart to be heard. Yes, the issue is critical, and losing arguments may be devastating. Also yes, I have resilience for distressing outcomes. True, other persons are perhaps more informed and articulate to engage a debate. Also true is the importance of my thoughts and feelings being expressed now. Listening to my authentic self guides me to befriend conflict and not get in the way of myself.

The *listening heart* also centers with others. I want to be clear about what someone is saying or trying to say. So I may need to delay reacting to a comment I find offensive or untrue. What is most important in the heat of conflict is for persons to be heard and understood. In a conflict with me, I will listen without having verbal or facial reactions that interrupt what the person is expressing. In a group conflict, this listening behavior can be stated as an expectation for honoring respectful discussion. The group can hold all members accountable to understand through attentive listening and respect.

After someone has spoken, a practice of restating what they have said can indicate that their comments are heard. They need not continue to repeat an argument for the sake of others' understanding. Questions might then be asked to clarify if they have been heard correctly. Questions of clarification are received differently than questions that argue or demean. For example, in conflict over neighborhood youth playing on church grounds, asking, "Are you concerned about the liability the church faces if there is an accident?" is completely different from asking, "Why do you not care about neighborhood children?" Questions should focus a group's ongoing discussion on stated positions in conflict, rather than on speculations about motives. Conflicts seething with the failure to listen, uncertainties about being understood, and expressed speculations about motives are a dangerous quagmire.

Listening attentively can result in seeing healing paths. I mediated a conflict between two women who had been best friends for years. However, for the last three years their friendship was dead. When one was in a financial crisis, the other had loaned her hundreds of dollars. As time and the financial crisis passed, the loan remained unpaid. The dispute over whether it was an unpaid loan or a gift had severed their relationship—except for ongoing demeaning comments and threats. As a last resort, they went to court; the court sent them for mediation.

I asked each to explain the conflict. The accusations were loud and angry. The bitterness was so thick that it was difficult to imagine they had been friends. Amid all the shouted details against one another, the woman who gave the loan said, "It's really not about the money. It's that you never thought enough of our friendship to work out a way for us to settle this. I trusted you! We had years of wonderful times together! And then, you treated me as you did!" She then continued to talk about the betrayal. When she finished, I focused on a comment like no other in her diatribe: "You said, 'this is not really about the money.' Tell me why you said that." She looked surprised to hear that she had said it. After a long pause, she told emotional stories about what her "former friend" had meant to her, and how invested they were in each other's lives. Now the former friend began to cry as she reminisced about their relationship and regretted that it had come to this. Without prompting from me, they began to laugh about past experiences together, tears flowed, an apology was given and accepted, and they embraced each other. With this new start to an old friendship, they said they could work out their conflict on their own. Contemplative listening befriends transformation.

⚜⚜⚜⚜⚜⚜⚜

Crossing identity boundaries with respect is essential to conflict transformation. The previous chapter noted sensitivities that need to be evident when entering another's realm of identity. Such sensitivities are also needed when speaking or displaying gestures about another's identity. Whether on the job, in church, in prison, homeless, or just walking down the sidewalk, persons you know or never met before will not only take affront at being disrespected; they may also react violently.

In his book *Resolving Identity-Based Conflict*, Jay Rothman explains why conflict based on group identity is more difficult to heal than interest-based (i.e., money, property, resources) conflict. His insights about conflict based on group identity also apply to conflict based on personal identity. He writes that "[Collective-identity conflicts] are deeply rooted in the underlying individual human needs and values that together constitute people's social identities, particularly in the context of group affiliations, loyalties, and solidarity." The issues in these conflicts are nonnegotiable. Rothman continues, "Identity-driven conflicts are rooted in the articulation of, and the threats or frustrations to, people's collective need for dignity, recognition, safety, control, purpose, and efficacy." Discussing situations where these different types of conflict exist, he writes, "it is fair to say that all identity conflicts contain interest conflicts; not all interest conflicts contain identity conflicts."[1]

We are wise to perceive when conflicts are fueled by identity matters. I have known rural churches with a dwindling membership to resist merging with another small-membership church of the same denomination. Both churches felt they were taking their last breaths before death. Still, they resisted befriending transformation for a promising future. In addition to the generations of precious memories that seemed bound to their current locations, each church's adjacent cemetery was so integral to their identity that merger discussions could not advance. The question "Whose building will become the congregations' home?" was equivalent to asking, "Who's willing to abandon their ancestors?"

Other identity issues can be more pronounced than the focus on cemeteries. Local churches have their distinctive cultures, which do not always harmonize with one another. The cherished responsibilities and authority that people have in their congregation may not transfer when joining another congregation. Worship services of the congregations may be conducted differently. In order to befriend transformation, a profusion of identity matters must be faced.

Being respectful and listening are essential to crossing identity boundaries. Hospitality is also a vital spiritual practice that befriends transformation. Table fellowship is an intimate act for nurturing relationships. Building trust in relationships occurs when significant time is spent together to demonstrate concern for one another, *personal stories* that portray common and different life experiences are exchanged, and those gathered have mutual experiences of being host and guest. The personal stories serve as portals that invite another into life narratives. Telling stories offers the privilege of experiencing another's heart. Relying on "persuasive" discussions to resolve conflicts embedded in identity is shortsighted. Hospitality helps to diminish anxieties about new relationships. Crossing identity boundaries with respect, heart-revealing stories, and hospitality bodes well for transforming conflict.

⚜ ⚜ ⚜ ⚜ ⚜ ⚜ ⚜

Befriending transformation is to *befriend the prophets*. The witness of prophets reminds and guides us to proclaim and enact God's vision of compassion and justice. Prophets are rightly accused of creating conflict. They embrace the accusation because the conflict they initiate is a faithful response to God's call. Prophets disrupt notions of peace that rely on suffering and oppression. Hope inspires and empowers the oppressed as it frightens and challenges guardians of the status quo. Frederick Douglass, the abolitionist credited as a major prophet against injustice, said:

> If there is no struggle, there is no progress. Those who profess to favor freedom, and yet depreciate agitation, are [people] who want crops without plowing up the ground. They want rain without thunder and lightning. They want the ocean without the awful roar of its many waters. This struggle may be a moral one; or it may be a physical one; or it may be both moral and physical; but it must be a struggle.[2]

Douglass's clarion call to activism is in the tradition of Jesus and the Hebrew prophets. We befriend transformation with humility and struggle . . . and without apology.

The transformation that prophets call forth is both reactive and proactive. Homeless families, senior citizens forced to choose between buying food and life-saving medication, children being sexually trafficked, and domestic violence are just a few of the heartbreaking crises on our watch. Fortunately, many organizations exist that react to the immediate needs that result from these crises. The organizations heal injuries and reduce misery. Accepting opportunities to contribute our time and finances is a caring *reaction* to crises.

Proactive transformation works at a different level. It endeavors to prevent suffering and injustice by changing how institutions and systems function. Advocating for this kind of change almost always involves conflict—conflict with diverse public opinions, with politicians disinterested in criticizing governmental institutions, and with officials responsible for operating institutions. For example, with over two million incarcerated persons, the United States has the highest per capita incarceration rate in the world. Accompanying the false belief that prisons are the means to a safer society is retrenchment from rehabilitation opportunities for inmates in order to increase the severity of their punishment. Politicians often blame increasing crime and high prison recidivism on the failure of prisons to be places of severe punishment. Caricatures persist of prison life as a comfortable experience where prisoners watch television, play sports, receive a free education, and are served sumptuous meals. The caricatures replace prison life's brutal and boring realities. Governments and prison authorities remove weight-lifting equipment, cancel college education and vocational training programs, limit library use, and cut budgets in mental health and chaplaincy programs as measures to assure the public that criminals are not coddled by the prison system.

Regarding the impact of prison educational programs, a RAND Corporation report concluded:

> Inmates who participate in any kind of educational program behind bars—from remedial math to vocational auto shop to college-level courses—are up to 43 percent less likely to reoffend and return to prison, the study found. They also appear to be far more likely to find a job after their release, and the social stability that comes with it.[3]

The Rev. Janet Wolf, whose SALT prison ministry was highlighted in the previous chapter, says that when the men in prison can read about, reflect on, and discuss critical social issues, a transformation occurs and individuals express, "Suddenly I imagine myself as a human being with a mind and I have power to engage the world."

Prisoners denied rehabilitation programs and services return to society less capable of finding legitimate work and functioning well. The violence, criminality, and mental-health stresses of prison increase the probability that released inmates will reenter society with more knowledge and experience of crime than ways to contribute to the commonweal. Society is unprepared for their release. Still, society fails to demand a more humane, safe, therapeutic, and skills-oriented prison system. When asked, "What are we doing about crime?" we point to prisons. When asked, "What are we doing about the problems prisons cause?" we point to plans for more prisons.

Without giving our hearts and resources to transforming the realities of incarceration, we either foolishly assume or pretend that more prisons are the answer for establishing our security.

Abundant opportunities exist for proactive transformation regarding incarceration. For example, we can challenge out-of-school suspension policies that release children to the streets of their precarious neighborhoods, advocate for alternatives to incarceration, join with groups speaking against excessive bail and sentencing, and support policies that eliminate barriers to employment for former prisoners. These are just a few of the many prophetic proactive transformation options.

With every issue, proactive transformation reduces suffering, is more cost effective than reactive efforts, and creates a more just society. Still, reactive care that requires immediate services to people suffering will always be needed. A homeless teenager needs safe shelter immediately, regardless of the responsible circumstances. Predators loom on the streets and act quickly. Both reactive and proactive transformation are necessary in beloved community.

❧❧❧❧❧❧❧❧

Chapter 5 spoke about the significance of preparation in being "journey bound." Attaining resources for anticipated ordeals is a wise decision. All persons, churches, and organizations will have conflict. This is certain. The question is, How will we prepare ourselves to befriend conflict and transformation? *Training in transforming conflict* is a wise and available answer.

Emphasizing the need for training is not an overreaction to conflict. Training is expected, whether you are a teacher, factory worker, firefighter, lifeguard, or are in some other profession where the absence of training could be damaging if not life threatening. If we have vowed to give our lives to healing suffering and injustice, and we know conflict to be both a threat to our efforts and a resource for our efforts, why do we resist conflict transformation training?

Yet churches do resist training in transforming conflict. I spoke with a longtime conflict transformation trainer of an organization that specializes in helping churches through crises of conflict. He said, "Churches call on us when they are embroiled in a conflict that divides the membership and causes people to go to other churches. We usually get called when they have exhausted their efforts to address the anger and frustration. What really disappoints us as mediators is the refusal of churches to pursue training before a crisis, and their refusal to request training after their current crisis is resolved." Befriending training is important to befriending transformation.

Imagine the difference for your congregation if leaders and others received training in conflict transformation. Even to have two or three members who are trained in procedures to honor diverse expressions and to prevent discussions from being stuck in noxious conflict can be especially reassuring when discernment occurs for prophetic neighboring. Members can also utilize their conflict transformation skills in service with community organizations.

Access to conflict transformation training is available. Internet searches provide descriptions of programs for individuals and groups. Some programs even focus on conflicts within religious institutions. You can also find conflict-transformation programs affiliated with denominations. If expense is a factor in pursuing professional trainers, churches could jointly sponsor training. The point here is that we have no excuse for remaining untrained. Training is a vital spiritual practice of preparation for justice and beloved community.

The ever-present need for skills in conflict transformation occurs even among people who have the same deep commitment to prophetic neighboring. Their conflict is not with persons opposed to initiatives for justice. Their conflict is with one another. Differences in naming priorities, strategic approaches, securing resources, leadership styles, assigning responsibilities, and a host of procedural matters can keep a group in turmoil. Transforming conflict skills are as essential for the group's internal viability as they are for the group's social activism.

I have been in meetings, both as a mediator and as a group member, where conflicts seemed intractable. Yet, with nonanxious and skillful befriending of conflict and transformation, I experienced healing and revitalizing miracles. Meetings began with no resolution in sight. However, trusting the conflict transforming *process* was crucial to dismissing unhelpful solutions or a premature decision to quit trying. *The process* of affirming respect, inquiring about personal and common desires for resolution, deep listening, restating what is being said so that persons know they are heard, and facilitating transitions that build confidence about the healing effort enable a reconciling spirit to grow and guide outcomes.

Important to the process is scheduling sufficient time. When people know that addressing their conflict is relegated to a brief time period or one attempt, they rush to be victorious before the meeting concludes. Persons will focus on asserting their feelings and persuading others, rather than listening and having their *discerning hearts* fully attentive.

The Rev. Janet Wolf's ministry with men in prison includes their training in mediation skills. Those trained have become so adept with their skills that prison guards have sometimes called on them to help when conflict has erupted on prison floors. Rev. Wolf spoke to me about one man involved in the training whose life was traumatized by his mother selling him for sex at age ten and giving him his first shot of heroin at age thirteen. After he completed conflict-transformation training, Rev. Wolf reports him saying that if he "had learned the mediation skills he now has, he would not have attempted suicide three times." The training transformed his life and gave him skills "to mediate the conflicts within himself." Training not only transforms external conflicts; it empowers us to befriend internal conflicts and our own transformation. *Hope is here in befriending transformation!*

Befriending Forgiveness

In the Gospel of Matthew (18:15–20), Jesus provides a procedure for addressing conflict between two persons. First, try to resolve the problem privately. If the offender does not "listen," involve others to verify the matters under dispute. Understanding that the conflict may continue because "that person refuses to listen to them," then bring the matter before the congregation. "And if the offender refuses to listen even to the church," then separate from the offender. Matthew cites Jesus as providing a procedure for churches to address their internal conflicts. Key to resolution is *listening*. If persons are not open to insight and authority beyond themselves, they cause the church's mission and work to be mired in disagreement. Some conflicts persist because minds and hearts are locked against perceiving afresh.

Continuing to recognize the effect of broken relationships for God's transformative work, Matthew writes: "Then Peter came and said to him [Jesus], 'Lord, if my brother or sister sins against me, how often should I forgive? As many as seven times?' Jesus said to him, 'Not seven times, but, I tell you, seventy-seven times'" (Matt. 18:21–22). The failure to forgive impairs personal relationships and community. Befriending forgiveness, therefore, is more than a gracious act toward another. Forgiveness is essential to the enlivening work of hope.

In Jesus' Sermon on the Mount (Matt. 5–7), he tells us to pray for forgiveness and to be forgiving. His instruction is straightforward and clear: befriend forgiveness. Again and again, Jesus instructs us with his words and his example. Again and again, we are inspired by his message, though we are uncertain if we can or even want to forgive. Praying for God to forgive us is not our quandary. What unsettles us is the command to forgive those who grievously offend us.

⚜⚜⚜⚜⚜⚜⚜

In 2006, when a gunman went into the one-room Amish schoolhouse and shot ten girls (ages six to thirteen) before killing himself, the world was horrified. Five girls died and another five were wounded. Their families and the Amish community were traumatized. The rest of us, shaken and grieving, tried to understand how this could happen. This unimaginable tragedy cast a pall over our imaginations. For days, all the "why" questions remained unanswered. Later attempts at explanation were senseless. The stories about the children were heart wrenching. Inspiring and heart wrenching was the story of the thirteen-year-old girl, Marian, who said to the gunman, "Shoot me first," in her hopefulness that it would save the others.

The response of the Amish community was inspiring and, for many in the country, bewildering. Amish parents and their community members expressed their immediate forgiveness for the gunman. They also went to the gunman's wife to console and offer her support. Everyone I heard on television and in personal conversations could not understand how they were willing to forgive—especially so soon.

In 2015, Black members of Mother Emanuel African Methodist Episcopal Church were in their Wednesday night Bible study. They welcomed a young White stranger who joined their circle. Near the end of their Bible study, the stranger pulled a gun from his fanny pack, declared that Black people were threats to the country, and began shooting the members. Nine died.

The world mourned. Protests erupted against the Confederate flag—a flag that symbolized pride in the slave-holding South. Stories about the hospitality of the Bible study group to the young stranger, the victims' caring lives, and the racial animus that fueled the crime were told and retold as the media was saturated with questions of "why?" and "what next?" The national need for healing was so deep that a memorial service for those killed was televised on all major channels and President Barack Obama delivered the eulogy.

When the shooter was arraigned in court for a bond hearing, three days after the killing, family members were given the opportunity to address him directly. Grieving their loss, in these widely reported statements they summoned their faith to express what needed to be said to the shooter, to the world, and to their own hearts:

> I will never talk to her ever again. I will never be able to hold her again. But I forgive you and have mercy on your soul. You hurt me, you hurt a lot of people, but God forgive you. I forgive you. (Nadine Collier, daughter of Ethel Lance)

> We welcomed you, Wednesday night, in our bible study with open arms. You have killed some of the most beautiful people that I know. Every fiber in my body hurts, and I'll never be the same . . . as we said in bible study, we enjoyed you, but may God have mercy on you. (Felecia Sanders, mother of Tywanza Sanders)

> She taught me that we are the family that love built. We have no room for hate, so we have to forgive. (Bethane Middleton Brown, sister of the Rev. DePayne Middleton-Doctor)

Some family members were not ready to announce forgiveness. Their unreadiness represented the reactions of many commentators I heard on television. The commentators walked a tightrope of respecting the faith commitment of grieving family members while also stating that forgiveness was given too soon and without holding the killer accountable. Commentators admitted that their own anger over the killings continued to rage. Expressions of forgiveness were heard by them as diminishing the significance of racism in spawning the killings.

Jesus' command to forgive is questioned in various ways—from disbelief to requiring contingencies of time and prerequisites. Befriending forgiveness is *essential* to befriending a future that is not plagued by unresolved hatred—from a past either distant or near. Knowing the purpose, power, and processes of forgiveness is vital to any future worth anticipating.

✤ ✤ ✤ ✤ ✤ ✤ ✤

For people of faith, forgiveness is fundamentally about being available to God, rather than being stuck in anger, bitterness, and desire for revenge. Revenge can motivate body and mind to wreak havoc on an enemy. Whatever satisfaction comes from its accomplishments will eventually sour before the gaze of our true selves. Revenge ultimately betrays who we are called to be for God and one another. Just as our personal lives falter from being driven by revenge, justice and beloved community do not arise from revenge.

God seeks to liberate us from enslaving emotions. Our true selves are nurtured with abundant opportunities to heal and grow—opportunities beyond the quagmire of hatred. Nations establish enriching cultural exchanges and economic development with former enemies, when they are not obsessed with forever punishing them. Forgiveness sets us free to devote our lives to hope's creative energies. As emphasized in previous chapters, we have agency with spiritual practices. Claiming and enacting our initiative to forgive honors the power God has given us to claim and enact our identity as God's freed people. When heading for the promised land, don't turn back to Egypt to settle scores.

Misunderstanding forgiveness impairs forgiving and the process of forgiveness. This occurs from insisting on *preconditions* to forgiveness. I've heard persons remark, "The Bible says we should forgive and forget. I can't forget what has been done to me, so I'm evidently not prepared to forgive." First, the phrase "forgive and forget" is not in the Bible. Ascribing it as a biblical injunction is an error. Second, people have traumas they neither can nor should forget. You do not forget a child being killed. You do not forget being gang-raped. You do not forget decades of false imprisonment. All these traumas may require extensive therapy to limit how the memories influence one's life. Forgetting, however, is *not* a prerequisite to healing and forgiveness.

Receiving an apology or a confession, behavior of repentance, or a request for forgiveness is the precondition that many people assert as necessary for forgiveness. When any of the preconditions occur, an injured person may be open to forgiving and to advance in their process of forgiving. Expressions of remorse can contribute to healing broken relationships—both personal and international. However, requiring expressed remorse as a precondition to forgiveness keeps the liberating act of forgiveness under the offender's control. An offender may not want to be forgiven. The offender may not want the injured to experience the release from anger and bitterness that forgiveness brings. If the offender is dead, and none of the preconditions is met, the injured remains captive to disabling emotions. Befriending forgiveness is our agency for our own healing. We can take the initiative to forgive, even when individuals and institutions fail to acknowledge their culpability in harming us.

In the Gospel of Luke, after Jesus had been beaten, falsely accused and condemned, crucified, and mocked, he prayed to God, "Father, forgive them, for they do not know what they are doing" (Luke 23:34). His petition that forgiveness prevail was not because his persecutors were remorseful and repentant. They were not. Perhaps he did not want their evil intent and folly to determine their future. I believe Jesus, suffering injustice and unimaginable physical agony, did not want to die with any bitterness residing in his heart. Jesus preached, "Love your enemies" (Matt. 5:44), and he would live his conviction to the end. Forgiveness is one of the powerful ways hope rescues us from despair.

Overcoming barriers to forgiveness also entails understanding what forgiveness does *not* mean. Forgiveness does not release a perpetrator from punishment for crimes and misdeeds. Forgiveness is not the willingness to now trust after a betrayal. Forgiveness is not being reconciled. Release from punishment, trust, and reconciliation are next steps that some persons and nations choose after they have forgiven. These choices, however, are not intrinsic to forgiveness. When we require needless preconditions before or mandatory acceptance after forgiveness is given, we build a daunting barrier between ourselves and forgiveness—a wall that deters forgiving.

Befriending forgiveness releases us from disabling emotions. The *process* of forgiveness may be immediate or may take years. No mandatory timetable exists for completing the process of forgiveness. Nor are we under the obligation to be done with issues of anger and grief once and for all. In the process of forgiveness, we can find ourselves needing to revisit issues we thought were settled. Still, as with physical health, our healing comes eventually from giving ourselves to the practices that free us from reopening old wounds.

Our being enlivened to life involves liberation from the oppressive power of revenge, bitterness, fear, and hate. Cultivating our forgiving capacities can also guide us in efforts to forgive ourselves. We harbor regrets about our own behaviors. We can be more than disappointed in ourselves; we can feel shame and alienation from our true selves. Forgiving others gives us lessons for forgiving ourselves. Forgiveness has this contagious affect.

⚜ ⚜ ⚜ ⚜ ⚜ ⚜ ⚜

I have listened to many sermons and Sunday-school lessons on the necessity for Christians to forgive. In these sermons and lessons, I never received instruction on *how to forgive*. Preachers and teachers advocated forgiveness as if hearing the command to forgive was sufficient for doing it. Our ongoing formation to honor our true selves, transform conflict, and become a people for beloved community involves knowing *how* to befriend the spiritual practice of forgiveness.

The Judeo-Christian tradition instructs through commands and stories. Chapter 2 of this book emphasized the significance of stories to faith formation:

> The work of hope has witnesses—some who live among us, and most who died long ago. They are authorities about its power to inspire us to "sing a new song." Their testimonies reveal and encourage. Listening and observing closely, we not only learn what hope has done for them, but also how hope may be working within us and others. Our becoming a people for justice

and beloved community relies on our entering their stories and being in fellowship with them. (page 30)

Reread this passage, replacing "hope" with "forgiveness." We have stories of witnesses who demonstrate the capacity and means to forgive. They inspire and instruct us.

When an Amish mother was asked how she could forgive so quickly the man who killed her daughter, I remember her saying, "All my life we were taught to forgive." In this heartbreaking tragedy, the guidance and comfort of her faith community sustained her. In the book *Amish Grace*, the authors explain how tradition helps to befriend forgiveness:

> Still, forgiveness probably comes easier for the Amish than it does for most Americans. Genuine forgiveness takes a lot of work— even *after* a decision to forgive has been made. Amish people must do that hard work like anyone else, but unlike most people, an Amish person begins the task atop a three-hundred-year-old tradition that teaches the love of enemies and the forgiveness of offenders. An Amish person has a head start on forgiveness long before an offense ever occurs, because spiritual forebears have pitched in along the way.[4]

Forgiving even "before an offense ever occurs" was included in the training of civil rights marchers. Dr. Bernard Lafayette, who worked with Dr. Martin Luther King Jr., told me that marchers were trained to forgive the anticipated abuse of police and White mobs *before* they marched. The nonviolence commitment of the civil rights movement had the spiritual practice of forgiving enemies as a prerequisite to protest. This would not only help marchers to refrain from a fight-or-flight reaction; forgiveness would steel their resolve to be nonviolent in demonstrating the power of love to overcome injustice. Forgiveness was an essential dimension of the nonviolent commitment to transform conflict.

The process of forgiveness is not one size fits all. Traumatic physical and emotional injury is complex. Consequently, prescriptions for healing vary, based on whether the injury was intentional or accidental, the extent of violation, the number of persons involved, cultural traditions, mental-health factors, expressed remorse, and myriad other factors important to those involved. Some prescriptions, like South Africa's Truth and Reconciliation Commission, require accountability and regret for violations. Sulha, a traditional Arab peacemaking process, involves families and communities in mediating conflicts between individuals, groups, and communities; the contributions of the larger community are considered essential for enduring peace. Martin Doblmeier's documentary *The Power of Forgiveness* focuses on the various ways individuals have forgiven and experienced forgiveness after dealing with murder, terror attacks, government neglect, the Holocaust, and other horrors to their loved ones. As part of Dr. Kiran Bedi's efforts to transform violence and prisoners' despair in India's prisons, she made Vipassana meditation (an ancient Buddhist practice) available to help prisoners forgive adversaries and to forgive themselves.

Three vital lessons emerge from this brief listing of examples that transform conflict by befriending forgiveness. First, the most harrowing deed is not beyond the power of forgiveness. The testimony from those involved in the most horrifying violations is a declaration of hope for victims, perpetrators, and communities. Second, each example has in-depth stories that we can enter through videos, books, and their storytellers. Inspiring instruction is abundant and accessible for us personally and collectively. Third, the capacity to forgive is not just for us to admire in people we regard as exceptional. The power of forgiveness is available to each of us. *Hope is here in befriending forgiveness!*

No Greater Love

In first-century Jerusalem, religious leaders and many people in the crowds opposed Jesus' teaching and challenged his authority. Conflict arose wherever he went. While eating with his disciples on this last night with them, Jesus was certain that death awaited. After the meal he continued to nourish them with instruction about love. He guided them to understand the significance of his sacrifice, as well as their own, when he said: "This is my commandment, that you love one another as I have loved you. No one has greater love than this, to lay down one's life for one's friends" (John 15:12–13).

Sacrifices for love of persons, country, and causes are life giving. Usually, these sacrifices take the form of extraordinary expenditures of time, energy, and resources to provide needed protection and sustenance for those we love. People risk death to assure their loved ones a future. A future worth anticipating is a future worthy of our total commitment.

Envisioning a future of compassion and justice can inspire us. Working for such a future will require us to befriend conflict. Transforming conflict will bring us friends and enemies. Some persons will oppose efforts for justice because they have a stake in the status quo. Advocating for reform in polluting industries, public safety policies, and discriminatory real-estate practices threatens their values and perhaps livelihoods. When you raise these issues in your community, the most dissenting voices may be coming from members of your church. Many guardians of the status quo are also active church members. Conflict flared when Jesus challenged injustices and authorities. Why should we expect otherwise in our efforts to befriend transformation in society?

Hope enlivens us to life beyond the consequences of conflict. Our prophetic remembering of God's dream to "let justice roll down like water and righteousness like an ever-flowing stream" (Amos 5:24) energizes us to love with every fiber of our being. Suffering, because of great love, always looms. Death, because of great love, is always a risk. Hope enlivens us with love to pursue whom God has called us to be for one another. When we are committed to the work of hope and love, the threat or even the certainty of death does not cancel our witness.

Père Jacques Bunol, was a Carmelite priest and teacher in a junior school in France during World War II. After the Nazis occupied France, he supported the underground French resistance and sheltered refugees and Jewish students. When friends cautioned him about the likely consequences from the Nazi occupiers, he responded: "Don't you think that if that happened, and if by chance I were shot,

I would thus be leaving my pupils an example that would be worth more to them than all the instructions I could give them?" After his arrest, he resisted initiatives to save him from prison camps by saying, "Priests are needed in prison."[5]

This all-in commitment puts suffering and death in their proper place as possible consequences. Rather than canceling prophetic witness, the role of suffering and death is limited to portraying what might happen. Sacrificial love is the transformative option that cancels the power of threats and fear to control us. Pursuing suffering and death is not the purpose of sacrificial love. Refusing to give suffering and death control over our steadfast love is a basic faith commitment for transformation. For Christians, when Jesus goes to Jerusalem, the vow to follow him is not up for revision. The specter of suffering and death may cause us to tremble; the specter should not cause us to stop. Beloved community relies on witnesses who insist and persist when conflict is protracted and even deadly. "No one has greater love than this."

⚜ ⚜ ⚜ ⚜ ⚜ ⚜ ⚜

Injustice is malignant. It spreads throughout society corrupting individuals and institutions. Whether we are rich or poor, privileged or oppressed, free or incarcerated, injustice is deadly. This deadly *fact* about injustice does not ignore that social groups benefit from injustice economically, politically, and in social standing. However, the benefits hoodwink many persons into thinking that all is well. First, the very soul of a society is enfeebled if society's institutions, laws, and community activism fail to be based on empathy for the poor and oppressed. Greed, dominance, and indifference are strong where empathy is weak. Second, injustice is like noxious clouds that blow across the landscape. The harm does not discriminate.

Prophetic remembering inspires us to transform injustice through conflict. The witness of abolitionists, labor organizers, human rights activists, and so many others provides instructive examples of transformation by sacrificial commitment. Love is the source of Jesus' description of sacrificial commitment as "to lay down one's life for one's friends" (John 15:13). Jesus also names love as the source for relating to adversaries. We are told, "Love your enemies" (Matt. 5:44).

Howard Thurman writes about nonviolence as a way of life and a strategic method that honors Jesus' belief that love should govern all human relationships—with friends, enemies, and strangers. Jesus' commitment is characterized by Thurman as the love-ethic. Thurman's insights influenced Martin Luther King Jr.'s adoption of nonviolence as the means to bring about social change. Thurman and King assert that the love-ethic is the only way the sacred worth of all involved in conflict is respected. Nonviolent activism does not demonize others. This activism endeavors to persuade oppressors and the oppressed that the goal is beloved community. Thurman writes:

> [The purpose of nonviolence] is to awaken conscience and an awareness of the evil of a violent system, and to make available the experience of the collective destiny in which all people in the system are participating. . . . The discipline for all who are involved has the same aim—to find a way to honor what is deepest in one person and to have that person honor what is deepest in the other.[6]

The well-being of the adversary is so paramount that nonviolent protesters choose to be unarmed when confronting adversaries with weapons. When conflict is so severe that the risk of suffering and death is acute, nonviolent activism is sacrificial.

Nonviolence is a method of the love-ethic. Dorothy Day, cofounder of the Catholic Worker Movement and peace activist, said, "Nonviolence makes the world safe for conflict." Day's statement and activism affirm the necessity for conflict, transformation, and the love-ethic. Without love as the source for nonviolent techniques, tyrannical regimes and repressive governments can use nonviolent techniques (e.g., counterprotests, art, books, music) to manipulate their citizens and perpetuate oppression. Techniques can be the means for both liberating and oppressive ends. Love is the defining motivation and ethic for transforming conflict, prophetic neighboring, and crossing identity boundaries for beloved community. Whatever hope accomplishes to enliven us to life is because we are also enlivened to love.

The apostle Paul's description of what love is and does inspires us. We are joyful and encouraged to know this force of God is in the world.

Love is patient; love is kind; love is not envious or boastful or arrogant or rude. It does not insist on its own way; it is not irritable; it keeps no record of wrongs; it does not rejoice in wrongdoing but rejoices in the truth. It bears all things, believes all things, hopes all things, endures all things. Love never ends. (1 Cor. 13:4–8a)

We experience fulfillment on our faith journey when we embody and enact love. Situations of conflict can be the most difficult times for expressing love. In conflict, energy is given to defense, acquiring advantage, accountability, demanding respect, survival, and expressing hate. Love seems untimely, if not irrelevant. However, befriending a future worth anticipating necessitates befriending love . . . always. Our efforts to transform conflict must include love. A successful outcome is not assured. Sometimes we remember that love is the best alternative only after our spirits are exhausted by protracted conflict and despair.

By demonstrating our commitment to love, we may persuade our combatants to continue our struggle on a path that leads to compassion and justice. Experiences of love can reset the ability of adversaries to see one another with increased respect for life. However, if our adversaries refuse to receive our initiatives of love, we can continue to witness to the ultimate significance of love through our sacrificial commitment—even our deaths. The options to love "never end." Perhaps we best perceive what love can do when we *fully commit* our lives to befriending transformation. *Hope is here in devotees of no greater love!*

❧❧❧❧❧❧❧

Transforming conflict can be a joy—not only in achieving successful outcomes, but also in the process itself. This chapter's emphasis on "befriending" is analogous to the respect, sensitivity, recognition of distinct attributes, dedication of time, and offering of oneself involved in our friendships. Befriending in personal relationships requires attentiveness and care that enable us to embrace friends with all their complexity. In struggles for justice and beloved community, respectful befriending with conflict, transformation, and forgiveness also requires attentiveness and care. Through befriending we perceive relationships, systemic realities, and ourselves with greater depth.

As stated throughout the chapter, befriending is the opportunity to be enlivened to life where conflict rages or needs to rage, transformation beckons, and forgiveness heals. Each of the spiritual practices—contemplative praying, prophetic remembering, crossing identity boundaries—is a resource for transforming conflict. The practices ready us for befriending opportunities. In addition, professional training is available to empower us as we offer ourselves to the work of hope. We can and must rely on love to always guide our commitment to transformation. Love is our motivation for befriending. Love dwells in conflict. Love empowers transformation. Love heals through forgiveness. Love leads us to offer our lives for God's dream of justice and beloved community. *Hope is here in transforming conflict!*

Questing with Questions

1. Reflecting on your experiences with conflict, assess your comfort in befriending conflict. Are you able to be creatively engaged when you are the subject of a conflict? What skills do you have to deal with interpersonal and systemic conflict? What skills do you need?

2. Whose approach to dealing with conflict do you admire? Why do they have your admiration?

3. When have you initiated conflict to address an injustice? Reflect on the possible consequences you weighed in making your decision.

4. What current injustice are you compelled to transform? What next step could you take for involvement?

5. Reflect on a relationship or situation when it was difficult for you to befriend forgiveness. If you were able to forgive, what was involved in your process of forgiving? If you were not able to forgive, what was the major obstacle?

6. Identify someone(s) you know personally whose ability to forgive an individual, group, injustice, or themselves is inspiring to you. What about their forgiving instructs you on how to forgive?

7. For what cause, if any, are you willing to risk your life? What motivates this commitment?

Chapter Seven

Celebrating Community

Life in community is no less than a necessity for us; it is an inescapable "must" that determines everything we do and think. . . . all life created by God exists in a communal order and works toward community.
—Eberhard Arnold, *Eberhard Arnold: Writings Selected*

In our communion, may we better understand what it means to be a creative, spirited community of healing, of hope, of resistance, and of transformation.
—Jan L. Richardson, *Sacred Journeys*

Where We Come Alive

"In the beginning is the image. In the image is the beginning." I began my book *Intimacy and Mission* with these words about the power of images for enacting mission. Images project stories, and stories involve us in realms of meaning. Our faith quest occurs with the benefit of biblical narratives, exemplary persons in religious traditions, and persons who portray the enlivening power of hope and love. They provide images that inspire and guide us to pursue a meaningful life—images that depict compassion and justice.

The images depict, *and they entreat*. As I said in chapter 2, "We look to the witnesses [biblical ancestors] as icons in our resourceful past, and the witnesses look to us as promise bearers for a fulfilled future. They long to see us give fuller expression to the work of hope. They encourage and urge us." We journey with ancestral and current witnesses as our companions. Our experience of community with them reaches across time and place. Our experience of community with them is for current times and places. Being a community inspired by God's dream for the earth, we work for justice and beloved community.

This chapter focuses on the meaning of community as God's gift to us. Community is essential for identity, purposeful living, and vitality. A future worth anticipating always includes creative energies committed to sustain these paramount functions of community. Understanding community's purposes also enables us to recognize suffering and to intervene in communities where oppression and injustice prevail. A vision of beloved community enlivens us to be activists for compassion and justice. Community is *where we come alive* to ourselves and our purpose in creation.

Community relies upon the renewing power of celebrations. Times of remembering, feasting, hospitality, Sabbath, and rejoicing nurture us personally and the communities that bind us to one another. Our prophetic witness is long term, with advances and setbacks. Our celebrating cannot wait until goals are achieved. Every step of our journey should be taken with an anticipated time for the renewing power of celebration. Celebrations are *where community sings* itself into new life.

Renewing community entails recognizing the *elements of celebration*. Sacred rituals need elements that root us in the present while transporting us to the past and future. For example, the water for our baptism touches us physically and emotionally as we remember Jesus presenting himself for baptism and our vows to be faithful witnesses. We receive and taste the communion bread and wine to feed a spiritual hunger as we "do this in remembrance" of Jesus and feel his abiding spirit as we move into our tomorrows. This chapter identifies essential elements for the transformative power of celebration.

The chapter concludes emphasizing the importance of celebration to *the essential nature* (fundamental attribute) of community. *Community is an organism*—an organism that requires stewards who tend to its vitality and growth. We are the stewards of this organism, and we must know *the true image of community* in order to bring forth community's creative purposes. If we misconstrue what community is, then we fail in our responsibilities for it. Celebrating a community made in the image of our anxieties and fears is idolatry. Idols, even gold ones, never take us to the promised land. Celebrating the true image and nature of community will enliven us for the journey.

⚜ ⚜ ⚜ ⚜ ⚜ ⚜ ⚜

In the beginning God created community. Genesis 1 tells of God speaking creation into existence. The creation of light and night, water and land, "vegetation: plants yielding seed of every kind and trees of every kind bearing fruit with the seed in it" (Gen. 1:12), living creatures "of every kind" (Gen. 1:20–25), and their ability to multiply. This community of life (in Gen. 1) preceded the creation of humans. In the second account of creation (Gen. 2), humans are created before the full flourishing of all other forms of life. In both narratives, God creates the world as a community of life that is essential for human flourishing. Community is where we are born and come alive.

The biblical narrative continues to stress community in the forms of family, tribes, nations, lands, religion, neighbors, exile, remnant, discipleship, and church. In all these forms, God seeks covenant relationship with God's people. Community was created to nurture us and to advance our coming into a right relationship with our Creator. God dreams of communities flourishing with pervasive compassion, righteousness, and justice. God desires for us to form and sustain communities that enact God's dream—for God's sake and our own sake.

Since our beginning (our births), we have required community. Our nourishment, security, and pleasure are not self-generated. Our dependence goes beyond food, security, and shelter, to being instructed on familial and communal identity, proper ways to be in relationship with others, and negotiating hazards of our environment. With maturity, we take increasing responsibility for our well-being and social character. But at no point in our lifetime have any of us been wholly self-reliant. Someone or something has provided, even in the most indirect way, resources from which we individually and communally have benefited.

Hermits are often cited in arguing that come adulthood, individuals do not need one another. This caricature fades when we know more about hermits. Ironically, hermits usually depend upon a supportive community of monks, neighbors, pilgrims, and even other hermits for food, resources, and protection. Before St. Celestine V became a pope, he led a community of hermits. I heard Bill Porter, author of the book *Road to Heaven: Encounters with Chinese Hermits*, speak about female Buddhist hermits in China who live in community in the mountains. Their dwellings are spaced apart; however, their proximity to one another provides protection. These hermits need food from villagers during difficult times. Stories are told about Christian hermits who through times of deprivation were sustained by food brought by ravens and other animals.

Even when hermits have been successful in self-care at every level of need, they have been indebted to those in the past. The journey of an individual is a journey taken with ancestors, teachers, and unknown contributors who, though long dead, are present in all that has made and is making the journey possible. The "communion of saints" is the term in many church traditions for the ongoing fellowship of the living and dead. We are created for and sustained by different forms of community.

⚜ ⚜ ⚜ ⚜ ⚜ ⚜ ⚜ ⚜

Not all communities are life-giving. Slave communities, abusive families, dysfunctional schools, congregations that relish turmoil, prisons withholding rehabilitation programs, and neighborhoods suffering benign neglect are dispiriting contexts. Yes, persons can emerge whole and hopeful from these realities. Individuals overcome great odds against their emotional, intellectual, and spiritual growth—and sometimes against their physical survival. Their resilience, however, does not diminish the damage done by cruel or dysfunctional communities. We rejoice when a grove of trees has survived a forest fire. Still, we should not be cavalier about the devastating loss of the forest, and neither should we ignore addressing the causes of the fires.

Too often the spotlights on resilient individuals fail to illumine the ongoing crises in their communities. The resilient individuals are touted as exemplary for what persons can achieve if they give sufficient effort. Persons who seem less resilient and remain damaged by their circumstances are then often accused of insufficient effort. The spotlight on individuals then becomes a reason to ignore the traumatizing realities of their communities.

Celebrating individuals whose determination and resilience inspire us is crucial to revealing the work of hope and to our being hopeful. However, we need to remember that their stories are always within a larger story about their communities. Just as chapter 4 emphasized our stewardship responsibility for our history, we have stewardship responsibility for communities. In Genesis 1:28, God says humans "have dominion over the fish of the sea and over the birds of the air and over every living thing that moves upon the earth." In other words, we have the responsibility to care for what God has given for sustaining community.

Care for "every living thing" and its environment is our charge. Regarding our own care, human community is as fundamental as land, water, and air. Our stewardship entails attention to whatever nourishes or threatens the vitality that God desires for us. Living in community can be experienced as "hell on earth" when society fails to give sufficient attention to address poverty, mental-health care, chemical addiction, religious bigotry that pits one religion against another, sexism, violence as a chosen remedy to conflict, and hostilities against people because of their sexual orientation and gender identity. These realities stifle beloved community. As we give ourselves to *celebrating community*, we are challenged to keep our hearts aware and responsive to sorrows that persist. Sometimes the celebrations acknowledge these sorrows. We require celebrations that prepare us to persist in our stewardship responsibilities to heal those who hurt and to transform our communities' oppressive realities.

⚜ ⚜ ⚜ ⚜ ⚜ ⚜ ⚜

Nature is the first community God created. Nature nurtures all communities. In this interdependent world, all communities are also responsible for nurturing nature. The environmental movement has detailed how our quality of life and our very survival depend on recognizing our roles in caring for the earth. Climate change affects weather patterns that affect crop growth that affects crop production that affects the food supply. Melting ice caps cause a rise in ocean levels that will overwhelm islands and seacoasts. Air pollution negatively affects the health of all life-forms. We have heard the warnings about how contamination of air, land, sea, *or* rivers becomes the contamination of air, land, sea, *and* rivers. The world is a community that is affected profoundly by the intraconnections of all its parts. My friend Cindy Farrar created a phrase that states how our perception of separation is an illusion: "No island is an island."

Our exposure to the elements of nature inspires and renews us. Whether the view is from a mountaintop, the rim of the Grand Canyon, or the ocean while at sea, we are overtaken by awe. Words fail to capture the experience. Description surrenders to reverence. John O'Donohue writes, "Nature was the first scripture, and at the heart of Celtic spirituality is this intuition: to be out in nature is to be near God."[1] The community that is nature is also where we come alive to God.

Our presence with Presence in nature is healing. When I asked the Rev. Janet Wolf (see chapter 5) about the spiritual resources that sustain her through the many heartbreaks that occur from her ministry in prisons, she responded, "I think primarily it's community. It really is the circles [groups comprised of men in prison, and professors and students from the seminary and college] that I'm a part of. . . . I really don't thrive without community." She then added,

> I do walks in the woods. I was walking this morning, and I'm walking in the same woods that I've been walking in since 1977. . . . And I'm leaving in the woods all the things that preoccupy me. And I'm building a room [in my spirit] as I have this morning with a chipmunk, some Catawba blossoms, and some moss on the side of a tree, and a cardinal, and I'm just filling up this room and it's stunningly beautiful, beauty all around me. . . . And those things that combine body, mind, heart, and spirit heal me so that I can go back to resistance against dehumanizing and unjust systems such as prisons.

In my interview with Fakhria (see chap. 5), I asked her how she dealt with the unexpected and devastating death of her brother during her first year in college. She mentioned that the college community's caring response was crucial to her ability to continue. The compassion expressed by professors and students meant a great deal for her healing. She then mentioned her time in the college's serene surroundings: "When I'm in nature, I forget about the conflicts, I feel calm, I feel peaceful. I cannot live without nature. . . . It's part of me because I'm so deeply connected with nature. Whenever I'm dealing with trauma, I spend time in nature." Community, including the community of nature, heals and enlivens us for the journey.

Celebrating nature is to revere its awe-inspiring power. Nature provides what is essential for our vitality. Air, water, land, vegetation, and animals are imperative for our survival. Also essential is the healing and transcendent power of nature's beauty. To celebrate nature as a cherished community means to live in it with gratitude and respect. In addition, celebrating nature means contributing to its health and well-being. Whatever we do to sustain the life in the community of nature also sustains us. More virtuous than the self-serving motivation is our commitment to be good stewards of the earth to delight God. *Hope is here in community where we come alive!*

Where Community Sings

Communities are organic. Like all organisms, human communities live and grow from nurturing environments. Human communities are generative and tend to give rise to individuals and new communities that embody their values. Our communities confront internal and external challenges to fulfill their reason to exist. The challenges exhaust some communities to death; other communities discover new life from their trials. As stewards of communities, we need to become knowledgeable about each community's particular needs and how we contribute to its thriving. Fundamental to our stewardship is enacting celebrations to enliven communities.

Celebrations are where communities sing. In chapter 1 I stated an African adage: "Before the spirit can descend, a song must be sung." Celebrations are where community members open their hearts to the transformative power of gathering, eating together, testimony about the journey, laughter, tears, rejoicing, and gratitude. These elements of celebration are ways our hearts "sing" our joy for the journey made in community. Consequently, a spirit overtakes our celebration that enlivens us anew to one another and our collective purpose. The spirit reminds us that more is with us than just us. Our anxieties diminish, our vision refocuses, and our imaginations and bodies are energized. Celebrations assure us of "our identity as community," and they intensify our commitment to community. Celebrations are where communities sing themselves into a future awaiting their witness.

✛✛✛✛✛✛✛

Giving our lives for justice and beloved community is a lifelong commitment. Community sustains us for the incessant challenges that come with transforming institutions and systems. Celebrations sustain community.

Celebrations are a form of communal Sabbath. They have so much in common that we can understand Sabbath as celebration and perceive celebration as Sabbath. Both provide a different rhythm to our arduous efforts to create, care, and transform. Regardless of how creative and productive we are day after day, we can feel detached from the ultimate purpose of our busyness. Sabbath and celebration are different from all the other times, and *they are needed for our fulfillment in all the other times*.

The Judeo-Christian tradition has stressed the importance of Sabbath as a designated day of the week with distinctive life rhythms that *celebrate* covenantal relationship with God. God's fourth commandment is the basis for this ritual time:

> Remember the Sabbath day and keep it holy. Six days you shall labor and do all your work. But the seventh day is a Sabbath to the LORD your God; you shall not do any work—you, your son or your daughter, your male or female slave, your livestock, or the alien resident in your towns. For in six days the LORD made heaven and earth, the sea, and all that is in them, but rested the seventh day; therefore the LORD blessed the Sabbath day and consecrated it. (Exod. 20:8–11)

The distinctiveness of Sabbath is stated as a day when the normal work activities cease for everybody, even livestock. Sabbath as a day to not work and to rest has led persons to describe Sabbath as "not doing." However, summarizing Sabbath as a time of rest fails to capture its full meaning. God rested on the seventh day, not because God was tired, but because God delighted in all that God had created. God blessed it. The Sabbath was a sacred day that marked fulfillment in God's creation and creating. Sabbath time completed (brought fulfillment to) all the other times of doing. The practice of Sabbath is a respite from routine, even as it reveals the holiness of routine. Although Sabbath is a time of rest *from* normal routines, New Testament scholar Clarence Jordan provides a more insightful understanding of *Sabbath as a time of zest.* Sabbath is a zestful time to come alive to who we have been, what we have done, and where we are going as God's people.

Celebrating community is a zestful time that recalls a community's identity, journey, and forthcoming promise. A community's past, present, and future convene. In this time of celebration, we are *not doing* problem-solving discussions, committee meetings, strategic planning, and budget analysis, which evoke anxiety. These matters remain; however, when we celebrate community, our attention to these matters is *at rest.* Celebration is a time to delight in God's sustaining power through all our successes and failures, the loss of community members and new persons joining, conflicts that threaten our serving together, anxieties that almost overwhelm us, and surprises that give us energy. After all this, in celebration we are now gathered to see one another, to rejoice in our privilege to serve, to thank God for the journey, and to continue the journey together. The celebration room has sounds of greetings, chatter, forks tapping plates, background music, and laughter. Words are spoken about who we are and what we have accomplished. Inspiring speeches are accompanied by a spirit-melody that is silent yet heard. All the sounds of the room become lyrics to a song that declares that we celebrate being community; and the spirit-melody accompanies all the sounds. This is where and how community sings in celebration and sings its way into the future.

⚜ ⚜ ⚜ ⚜ ⚜ ⚜ ⚜

Celebrations are a form of spiritual retreat *from and for* our creative efforts as witnesses for justice and beloved community. The need for everyone to *anticipate* a renewing time of retreat from usual routines was revealed in my conversation with a Benedictine monk as we ate lunch together at his monastery. I asked about his personal journey to monastic life and the work of the monks. When I inquired about the daily schedule for the monks, he said they awoke early in the morning hours and that many monks used this time for prayer. Breakfast was at 6:30 a.m., followed by Morning Prayer at 7:00 a.m. Monks then went to their various work responsibilities around 8:15 a.m. and ended this work in time to prayerfully read the Scriptures by 11:30 a.m. This was followed by Midday Prayer and then lunch. About 1:15 p.m. the monks returned to their work. At 4:30 p.m. they again prayerfully read the Scriptures. Mass was celebrated at 5:00 p.m. Dinner was served at 6:00 p.m., and Evening Prayer started at 7:00 p.m. After Evening Prayer, the monks had a twenty-minute period called Evening Quiet. The rest of the evening was for whatever they chose to do until the 10:30 p.m. Night Silence. The Saturday and Sunday routines had slight variations in worship times.

As I listened to this schedule, I was impressed by their dedication to pray, worship, and study Scripture throughout the day. Each day was devoted to routines that deepened their lives to the presence of God. After the monk had spoken about his day's schedule, his body straightened, a smile broke across his face, and he said something that made an even bigger impression than his recitation of the daily routine. He said, "And I can't wait until August." I asked, "What happens in August?" He replied with sheer delight, "In August, we go on retreat." To this day I have wondered if my face betrayed the surprise I felt from his response. I thought, How can this monk long for a time of spiritual retreat when every day of his life is a routine of spiritual deepening? Yet he and his religious community were anticipating a different kind of prayerful time. They needed it, and knowing that it awaited them enlivened their ordinary days of routine.

By analogy, our work for justice and beloved community can be fulfilling. We experience zest from contemplative praying, prophetic remembering, crossing identity boundaries, and transforming conflict. The spiritual practices guide and empower us on this long journey. Still, we long for a furlough from the usual routines of our witness. To be clear, this is *not* a furlough *from* the journey, but a furlough *for the spiritual practice of celebration.* We need to hear community sing a different zestful tune. Whether the celebration is marked on a calendar or is being conceived in discussions, even anticipating celebrations enlivens us anew. *This transformative power of celebrations is then extended to the present time.* Just to anticipate celebrations is to experience hope.

Celebrations continue to abide with us beyond their benedictions. We remember and relive inspiring moments from festive times. A phrase from a speech or prayer, the emotions that overwhelmed efforts to speak, an unexpected embrace from a coworker, a song that our hearts continue to sing, and the community feeling of being one-in-the-spirit are ways celebrations go into the future with us. *Hope is here in celebrations where community sings!*

Elements of Celebration

Not every event in the name of "community celebration" is enlivening. At some point during a celebratory event, we may keep checking the program and our watches for the benediction to release us. But communities pursuing justice and beloved community require enlivening celebrations to sustain their witness. Communities *need* zest. They *need* to sing, because post-celebration challenges await communities. Soon, fatigue will again plague the most active community members. Financial stability seems never assured. Some relationships must be healed. The ever-evolving realities of injustice demand different strategic approaches. The vision being pursued requires attracting new workers. The zest from celebrating invigorates us to meet these challenges for beloved community.

Our spiritual practices are vital to planning and enacting community celebrations that inspire us for tenacious activism. *Contemplative praying* deepens our efforts to envision and prepare a celebration. Our listening hearts are then attuned to the desires, needs, anxieties, and joys the community has expressed. This listening helps us to prioritize our goals for the event. For example, a coalition of faith and neighborhood organizations may feel defeated when months of exhausting activism do not result in policies that limit out-of-school suspensions. The research data was clear that these suspensions result in children being less capable to complete their education. The meetings with school officials seemed promising. Still, nothing changed. Upon hearing the increased cynicism from community members about the ability to affect transformation, we know that a goal for the upcoming celebration will be to defeat defeatism.

The event can both acknowledge disappointment *and* be festive. The gathered community can be inspired to hear how members are more informed and organized than when they began. Rousing speakers can remind everyone that abandoning the children is not an option. The struggle must continue, and persistence will prevail. Humorous stories about missteps and awkward incidents can lighten the mood, as laughter becomes an antidote to disappointment. The food energizes bodies and spirits. The music proclaims we have joyful rhythms and lyrics that carry us. Including children as speakers and singers transforms the event from references *about* children to *seeing and hearing* children open their hearts to the community for a loving response. Children's belief that the future holds promising opportunities inspires a community to advocate for those opportunities. If our *listening hearts* are attuned to the community, our *discerning hearts* are more likely to envision and plan an enlivening celebration that empowers our *engaging hearts* for the ongoing struggles for justice and beloved community.

Prophetic remembering brings our faith ancestors into our celebrations. The prophets' visions and messages for compassion and justice inspire our witness. The prophets remind us that God's sorrow and anger must also be the community's sorrow and anger. Whether we rejoice in victorious outcomes or lament devastating defeats, our communities' unrelenting focus on responding to the vision and work for beloved community is itself cause for celebration. Consequently, enlivening celebrations cast the prophetic vision that depicts a community's purpose, inspires commitment, and stimulates resilience. Portraying the prophetic vision through event invitations, community testimonies, and the arts are ways that prophetic remembering becomes evident in a celebration. I have experienced celebrations where *the gathering* of people from various faith traditions, races, ethnicities, generations, and economic statuses *became the prophetic vision*.

Crossing identity boundaries both creates and celebrates community. Our faith and cultural differences too often separate us from heart-to-heart experiences with one another. The separation fuels alienation. Even though we may live and work in the same community, we often fail to have relationships with each other that enliven us to our oneness as community members. Celebrations can awaken us to community through activities that foster our crossing identity boundaries.

Through my involvement with the Interfaith Children's Movement (ICM), I became aware of the horrors experienced by sexually trafficked children. ICM worked with individuals, faith communities, and organizations to increase public awareness and to advocate for legislation that aimed to prevent sexual trafficking. Years of public meetings and legislative advocacy were filled with increased public support, but disappointing legislative outcomes. However, with insistence and persistence that public notices about sexual trafficking be displayed in the airport, hotels, and entertainment venues, we achieved the first of many changes to come. Eventually, laws were passed that increased the punishment of persons involved in the sexual exploitation of children. An amendment to the Georgia Constitution was passed to collect fees that would fund rehabilitation services for sexually exploited children. Our successful activism relied upon celebrations both in times of defeat and in times of success.

A major annual celebration was the Anti-trafficking Passover Seder cosponsored by ICM and several synagogues. Hundreds of us gathered in a synagogue's meeting hall to participate in this Jewish ritual that celebrates God's liberation from enslavement. We were Jews, Christians, Muslims, Buddhists, Bahá'ís, Unitarian Universalists, and likely some who self-identified as nonreligious. The Seder ritual was adapted to address contemporary human trafficking realities. We recited together both Hebrew Scriptures and Passover themes that spoke to our common commitment to resist enslavement. We ate the Passover food elements on our tables as we heard how each item symbolized a sacred theme for the journey from slavery to freedom. Waiting for us was a sumptuous meal that was kosher and halal to honor the dietary laws of Jews and Muslims. Our conversations at the multifaith tables were personal and religious.

The Seder celebration was a crossing of identity boundaries for everyone. Our common conviction to end human trafficking had brought us together. The Passover Seder took us into a particular religious tradition that spoke to the gathering of many different identities. We entered the room as an issue-centered community. We left the celebration with a new sense of community that was inspired by our experiences of crossing identity boundaries. The event both celebrated community and enlivened us to an expansive understanding of what community means.

Community celebrations can also help in *transforming conflict*. Internally for a community, planning a celebration can shift members' energies from battles over advocacy and programmatic strategies to hosting a celebrative time. They are *not* forsaking matters that need resolution. The work given to enact and experience a celebration, however, shifts energies to portray prophetic vision, express hospitality to familiar and new relationships, create a joyous time, and trust in God's abiding presence. After the celebration, adversaries return to disputed matters with renewed energy and a spirit of cooperation for addressing what were inflexible positions.

Celebrations are also the opportunity for community organizations and churches to transform conflict with persons and groups that have opposed their efforts for justice and beloved community. For example, a group of churches with ministries to their homeless neighbors invited local residents and business owners to celebrations about their outreach ministries. The invitations were an effort to overcome the hostility that some residents and business owners felt toward a church's outreach programs. The hostility was based on the belief that these programs were a magnet that brought increasing numbers of homeless persons into the neighborhood—along with increased loitering, debris, begging, . . . and fewer customers.

One church's approach to invitations began with personal conversations that connected residents and business owners with a church member or pastor. The conversations established a relationship with those invited, rather than relying on mailers to encourage attendance. The invitations made clear that the celebration event would not be a time to confront one another about the ministries. The event's purpose was to overcome the alienation and misunderstanding among the different groups who constituted the neighborhood.

Stated positively, the purpose was to come together as caring neighbors for one another.

The celebration acknowledged all who attended—church members, residents, persons who were homeless, business leaders—and stressed their significance to a vital neighborhood. Selected attendees gave testimonies about their meaningful relationships with one another—testimonies that portrayed one another as caring rather than as threatening. Crucial to the celebration was also acknowledging the concerns that kept the neighborhood from being a welcoming, clean, and vital place for everyone. The celebration *was not* planned as the event that would solve all the conflicts between the churches and their neighbors. Transforming the conflicts would require several scheduled meetings that clarified issues, offered proposals, considered acceptable compromises, and sustained the commitment to respect one another as neighbors. The celebration, however, *was* planned as an essential phase of the transforming conflict process.

⚜ ⚜ ⚜ ⚜ ⚜ ⚜ ⚜ ⚜

In addition to the spiritual practices, renewing community through celebrations relies upon *food, beauty, gratitude, and trust*. A celebration without these elements will likely feel that something essential is missing for the event and for activism after the celebration.

Food is a sign of hospitality. A display of tables with food and drinks announces, "We have prepared for your arrival and comfort; welcome to this gathering!" Food reflects a host's sensitivity to the needs of guests. In an interfaith gathering, dishes are available for guests whose religions have dietary restrictions. Vegetarians have meatless options. If food is a buffet, hosts can engage guests in conversation as they identify buffet items. Valuing a person-to-person connection is demonstrated even in how food is offered.

Celebrations where potluck dishes are the meal spur conversations about ethnic and regional offerings, favorite family recipes, and cooking methods. Food launches stories that become a portal into personal and family histories. Conversations about food celebrate personal and cultural identity. Table fellowship is not only a place to enjoy food and conversations; it can initiate meaningful and ongoing relationships.

Beauty transports celebrations to inspiring heights. Multiple forms of beauty enliven us. Music inspires some to nod and others to sing and dance. Poetry with metaphors takes us to depths of meaning beyond words. Paintings portray crises and compassion. Room and table decorations manifest that this is a festive time. What is seen, heard, and absorbed tells everyone that when the event planners gathered, beauty was at their table.

Exhibiting beauty may draw upon the gifts of community members. In addition, the need for beauty may lead planners to invite contributions from artists who previously had not been involved with a community's activism. Since all movements for justice depend on artists to depict the struggle, the artists' involvement in the celebration may prompt them to contribute to post-celebration activism.

Psalm 150 discloses how our spiritual ancestors used their bodies and instruments to celebrate God's greatness. Praise is expressed through artistic beauty:

> Praise him with trumpet sound;
>   praise him with lute and harp!
> Praise him with tambourine and dance;
>   praise him with strings and pipe!
> Praise him with clanging cymbals;
>   praise him with loud clashing cymbals!
> Let everything that breathes praise the LORD!
> Praise the LORD!
>
> (Ps. 150:3–6)

Beauty comes through us to express our rejoicing hearts.

Whether in nature or language or the arts, beauty is God's gift to us. Beauty evokes perceptions and feelings that cause us to praise God and be aware of God's abiding presence. The transformative power of beauty heightens our consciousness of transcendent meaning and wonder. As Annie Dillard writes, "Beauty is not a hoax."[2]

In addition to beauty created by God and human invention is the beauty of the compassionate life. Caring relationships are beautiful.

We are inspired when we witness love enacted. Our spirits take flight, tears may flow, smiles come forth, and we are blessed by the heart-warming radiance of love. Evelyn Underhill, in her groundbreaking book *Mysticism*, writes about mystics who perceive "harmony" with "life in all its forms." Beauty is perceived through the prism of love. Underhill writes: "All things are perceived in light of charity, and hence under the aspect of beauty: for beauty is simply Reality seen with the eyes of love."[3] *Transformative community celebrations provide attendees with a vision of a community's love.* Love is beautiful, and beauty reveals love. The ultimate significance and transformative power of beauty led Fyodor Dostoevsky's character Prince Myshkin to assert: "The world will be saved by beauty."[4]

Gratitude conveys a community's appreciative heart. A grateful community sees and acknowledges those who constitute the community. In a community celebration, whether written on a program or spoken from the podium, persons anticipate being acknowledged for their contributions to the work of the community and the celebration event. Expressions of gratitude tell persons, "You are seen and remembered and appreciated." No one wants to be taken for granted.

Celebrating community with expressions of gratitude cultivates loyalty. More important, expressing gratitude nourishes a community's heart for beloved community. Gratitude is a dimension of caring relationship. At a level deeper than "we are thankful for what you *do*," gratitude says, "We are thankful for *who you are*." When celebrating community affirms persons, in addition to their contributions, a spirit of love characterizes the community. Gratitude for one another persists, whether efforts succeed or fail. Gratitude for the community persists, whether advocacy for justice is victorious or defeated. Gratitude for God persists in seasons of communal harmony and in seasons of turmoil. Celebrating community relies upon gratitude that is energized by love. Without genuine expressions of love, communities are prone to idolize achievement as the primary basis for celebrating community. The contributions of community members are uplifted as the homage given to the idol of achievement. The absence of gratitude for persons and for God results in coldheartedness, which fails to lead us to experience beloved community.

Trust is an element of community that determines if working relationships are characterized by assurance or suspicion. Community members' ability to trust one another in service to a community's mission is important. However, the chapter's emphasis here is on our *trust in God in celebrating community.*

Planning a community celebration can be rife with anxiety. The celebration may have objectives that are considered pivotal to the future success and even existence of a community. Major questions about the upcoming celebration pervade. Will the event be a healing experience for wounded relationships in the community? Will invited guests come? Will we meet crucial fundraising goals? Will hearts be inspired by the community's work and this celebration? Will the featured speaker arrive? Will the event's attendance be affected by weather?

The questions bespeak the multitude of matters beyond a community's control. The lack of control is a source of anxiety. The mounting anxiety caused by uncertainties drains energy and wastes time without controlling the uncontrollable. Trust in God enables a community to pursue its purpose without the burden of anxiety. This trust is more than belief about God. Trust is a level of assurance that releases us from the false notion that anxiety causes good outcomes. Our nervous system can then be devoted to pursuing the work and experiences of God's beloved community.

In the Gospel of Matthew, Jesus teaches about rejecting anxiety. He says,

> "Therefore I tell you, do not worry about your life, what you will eat or what you will drink, or about your body, what you will wear. Is not life more than food and the body more than clothing? Look at the birds of the air: they neither sow nor reap nor gather into barns, and yet your heavenly Father feeds them. Are you not of more value than they? And which of you by worrying can add a single hour to your span of life?" (Matt. 6:25–27)

Worry is unproductive and a distraction from where our energies should be given. Concerns we have about our fundamental needs merit our attention and effort, but not our anxiety. Jesus concludes this message saying, "Indeed your heavenly Father knows that you need all these things. But seek first the kingdom of God and his righteousness, and all these things will be given to you as well" (Matt. 6:32–33). God knows and God cares. As I stated in chapter 2, the most fundamental question of the spiritual journey arises when we feel anxious and in need of assurance: "Do I *trust God* with my life?"

In preparing to celebrate community, this question is hopefully turned into a declaration through prayers, planning discussions, and the spirit of working together for a celebrative event: "We trust God for this celebration for our community!" Freedom from anxiety liberates our energies to pursue the work of celebration. All aspects of preparing for the event are done with a sense of God's supportive presence. The joy of celebrating community is then not delayed until the event occurs; the joy begins with preparation.

Trust does not guarantee that the celebration will fulfill all the community's needs and expectations. Even the best preparation efforts can result in disappointing outcomes. Righteous causes experience one disappointment after another. Still, we can rejoice that we have "run with perseverance the race that is set before us" (Heb. 12:1). We rejoice in knowing that God is with us and providing what we need in disappointing seasons. Celebrating community continues after the celebrative event. Whether our emotions are high or low, being amid a community that devotes itself to trusting God uplifts us to continue running with perseverance. Hope enlivens us to the ongoing journey, in times of joy and disappointment, through God's gift of community that has been *entrusted* to us.

✿✿✿✿✿✿✿✿

Celebrating community in traditional and innovative ways acknowledges the transformative power of celebration in honoring a community's past and preparing for its future. Celebration is not a frill. We focus our energies to discern what needs to occur for a celebration to inspire a community. We call upon God to use us to bring forth what we yearn to achieve in celebrating community—as well as blessings we had not even envisioned. Our effort to address what a community needs will produce a multitude of celebration options for discernment. We are wise to include the elements of celebration in our planning and festivities. *Hope is here in the elements of celebration!*

The True Image of Community

This chapter began by discussing the power of images, and how beloved community relies on a vision of community that enlivens us to be activists for compassion and justice. An image of community must align with the fundamental facts of how communities function—in other words, understanding the basic nature (the life characteristics) of communities. Knowing the basic nature of communities is crucial to our being their faithful stewards.

We must see the *organic nature* of communities. They have a perpetual need for nourishment. Nourishment comes from sufficient food, healthy economies, needed technology, educational opportunities, justice for all, and attention to the myriad matters that threaten communal vitality. The organic nature of every community means communities are forever changing. Even monastic communities based on "stability" cope with the various and changing personalities of monks, different interpretations of rules, problems with obedience, illnesses that disrupt usual responsibilities, deaths, novitiates, natural disasters, pilgrims, guests, and tensions with surrounding property owners—and these are just a few of their ongoing realities. All communities are in some form of change that requires tending.

When we image community as organic, we can then align our expectations and involvement with the image. The organic image prevents us from working on behalf of community with the false notion that some adjustment will *fix community once and for all*. Communities are never "fixed." Families, congregations, schools, neighborhoods, nations, and empires are never fixed for all time. Like every person, the organic nature of communities is dynamic. Organic images of community will pulsate success and failure, growth and decline, joys and sorrows, generosity and greed, wisdom and folly, loving-kindness and cruelty. If we conjure images of communities that are contrary to their organic and dynamic reality, our intentions to effectively care for communities will be engulfed in frustration, bewilderment, and despair.

In addition to organic images of communities, the image that most motivates our activism and celebration of community is the image of beloved community. Just as the "true self" discerns and informs the "self" of every person (see chapter 3), the image of beloved community informs our activism for community and inspires our celebrating community. *Beloved community is the true image of community.* Our "true selves" so resonate with this "true image" of community that we are enlivened to create experiences of beloved community. The organic complexity of communities is daunting. Still, we have means to bring forth experiences of beloved community that sustain us and our communities with joy. Hope enlivens us to listen/discern/engage prayerfully, remember prophetically, facilitate the crossing of identity boundaries, transform conflict, and celebrate community.

This whole book has presented experiences of beloved community. They occurred in dining rooms, worship services, church outreach programs, homeless shelters, schools, protests, conversations, prisons, responses to massacres, nature, and celebrations. The impact and significance of beloved community experiences are easily missed and dismissed. We may not perceive beloved community if we expect a beloved community experience to eliminate causal problems or to *fix* a community. Our hearts are destined to be cynical and disparaging if a beloved community experience must meet such expectations. The enduring impact of compassion and justice is then lost to myopic desires for continuous progress and change that is permanent.

New Testament stories of Jesus proclaiming and enacting God's dream of compassion and justice depict beloved community experiences. Jesus has intimate relationships with outcasts. People suffering infirmities are healed. Hungry crowds are fed. Persons burdened by their sinfulness are forgiven. The poor and oppressed are inspired by prophetic messages of God's liberating love. The authority of religious and governing leaders is threatened by Jesus' opposition to their oppressive rule. Experiences of beloved community occur as Jesus enlivens people with the power of love and hope.

Continuous progress and permanent change are *not* outcomes from Jesus' ministry. Outcasts continued to be disparaged and shunned. Everyone whom Jesus healed eventually died. People whom Jesus fed still had days of hunger. Persons forgiven of their sins faced new challenges to live righteous lives. The poor and oppressed continued to live in poverty and oppression, even as they responded to an uplifting prophetic vision. Religious and governing leaders executed Jesus and tried to eradicate his followers. If we discount Jesus' compassion, healing, and prophetic witness because these expressions of beloved community did not result in permanent personal and cultural changes, then all visionary and holy transformations are futile. I pray that we are wiser than to fall prey to such a soul-crushing delusion.

Beloved community experiences can be brief and transitory, yet still have an enduring significance on the present and future. Jesus' response to God's calling upon his life has inspired compassion, healing, and prophetic witness over the centuries. The significance of our efforts for beloved community will also endure within and beyond our lifetimes.

Recognizing that experiences of beloved community are occurring around us, to us, and through us makes our hearts eager to celebrate community. The celebrations, both personal and communal, affirm that we are blessed to perceive the true image of community. Our joy does not wait for experiences of community where progress is permanent. We are enlivened by experiences of beloved community that hope and love bring forth *now*! We are enlivened by our opportunities to become a people who dwell with the true image of beloved community.

⚜ ⚜ ⚜ ⚜ ⚜ ⚜ ⚜

In Paul's First Letter to the Thessalonians, he praises them for their steadfast witness as followers of Jesus, and he exhorts them to "lead a life worthy of God" (1 Thess. 2:12). In the Second Letter to the Thessalonians (a letter that many scholars doubt can be attributed to Paul), the message continues to proclaim the themes in the first letter. After noting how others are failing to live according to what Jesus requires, the writer instructs and encourages the community by saying, "Brothers and sisters, do not be weary in doing what is right" (2 Thess. 3:13).

This is wise instruction—especially if the writer means *do not forsake or choose to withdraw* from doing what is right. However, if the writer means do not become tired or exhausted in doing what is right, then this counsel is problematic. Exhaustion in doing what is right is a natural human outcome. Weariness is an organic fact from exerting energy. The failure to address weariness creatively can lead to a physical, emotional, and spiritual crisis.

Yes, doing what is right can be energizing. We experience joy that comes from devoting our time and hearts to the nurture of a child. An empowering feeling comes from seeing legislation passed that we have worked on for years to guarantee the rights of persons who have suffered discrimination and injustice. Caring can be so inspiring and transformative that we often say, "The reward from caring is caring itself." We also become weary in doing what is right—more than weary, exhausted. Sometimes, more than exhausted, we become distraught—at times, even despairing. Activism for and in beloved community takes a toll.

Care for the caring is crucial to sustaining the work of compassion and justice in community. Some caregivers expend themselves caring for others every hour of every day of every month of every year without anticipating any time for renewal: parents caring for severely disabled children; adult children caring for parents with dementia; parents working two or three jobs, who come home to draining demands from their households; community activists without the financial resources to attend renewing conferences with other activists; persons who feel unacknowledged and without significant support as they conduct after-school and summer programs for youth, attend to the needs of homeless persons, or advocate for employing the formerly incarcerated.

Care for the caring is needed wherever persons are "doing what is right," yet their "doing" leaves them overcome by relentless fatigue. *Creating restorative experiences for caregivers and advocates is another way to celebrate community.* The healing relief given to caregivers by individuals, churches, and organizations may seem inadequate in light of the constant time and energy demands caregivers confront. However, restorative experiences bestowed by a caring community will enliven them and persist with them for the coming journey. *Hope is here in the true image of community!*

⚜ ⚜ ⚜ ⚜ ⚜

Celebrating community is a portal experience to the work and joy of beloved community. The celebrations reveal the longings of our hearts and how we have lived and worked together in response to God's dream for us. I've stated, "Celebrations are a form of communal Sabbath." Like Sabbath, celebrations are arrival at an anticipated time of thanksgiving, praise to God, fellowship, and renewing rituals that empower us for the days ahead. Like Sabbath, celebrations occur for both present and coming times. Like Sabbath, our full availability in times of celebration can prepare us for the new ways God meets us in beloved community.

By analogy to this last insight, Rabbi Solomon of Karlin speaks of Sabbath as a foretaste of heaven:

> Unless one learns how to relish the taste of Sabbath while still in this world, unless one is initiated in the appreciation of eternal life, one will be unable to enjoy the taste of eternity in the world to come. Sad is the lot of him who arrives inexperienced and when led to heaven has no power to perceive the beauty of the Sabbath.[5]

Celebrating community can be an experience of beloved community, and the celebrations can empower our witness for beloved community. We become more attuned to what God has done, to what God is doing, and to God's abiding love in times to come.

This chapter stresses the role of community as God's gift of a place *where we come alive*. With the gift comes our responsibility to be stewards who care for the organic nature of community, so that our communities fulfill God's nurturing and transformative purposes for us and the world. Our stewardship includes preparing celebrations to remember the journey with God, to cherish the blessings of relationships, and to be inspired for the coming journey. *Celebrations are where community sings.* As a spiritual practice, celebrating community should include essential elements as resources for planning celebrative events and portraying a community's heart. *The true image of community* (beloved community) emerges through celebrations with hospitality, testimonies of compassion and justice, beauty, expressions of gratitude, relationships of trust, and care for the caring. *Hope is here in celebrating community!*

❧❧❧❧❧❧❧

Hope enlivens us to the meaning of love in community. The more we engage the diverse realities of communities, the more we are challenged by the complexity of communities as they exist—*not just as we wish communities to become.* Each of our communities, those in which we live and those we need to join by crossing identity boundaries, is where our hearts yearn and learn for our true selves to be engaged with love. God's force of love is with us and comes through us for our becoming whole for beloved community. Yes, this is love for friends and kin. This love pursues fulfillment in our relationships with strangers, enemies, those we do not like, those who do not look like us, those who do not think like us, those who do not believe like us, and those who neither like nor love us. Beloved community is a place where we strive to love others as God loves all of us.

I do not believe that we grasp fully the extent and depth of this love. When hope enlivens us to life, we are enlivened to love's transformative and unfathomable power. Even as we declare love as essential to God's dream of justice and beloved community, love surpasses our understanding. Love is a sacred mystery. Love is not a mystery for us to solve, but a mystery for us to revere, embrace, and enact in all our days.

For a people on their faith journey with Jesus, every step is guided by God's inspiring dream of beloved community. Every step leads to opportunities to do justice and be compassionate. Every step can be taken walking humbly with God. The assurance of God's abiding presence and love makes every step a doxology: Praise God from whom all blessings flow.

Questing with Questions

1. In which communities (e.g., family, church, social organizations) do you currently feel most nurtured to contribute to justice and beloved community? Indicate why you selected the community (or communities). If no community comes to mind, what next steps might you consider?
2. Reflecting on community celebrations that you recall with joy, what occurred that continues to inspire you?
3. Have you planned and/or attended a community celebration about activism for justice? If so, what elements of that celebration addressed your faith and commitment? How did the celebration influence your involvement in the justice issue?

4. Reflecting on your experiences of celebrating community, which of the spiritual practices (chapters 3–6) were most prominent in the inspiring celebrations? Comment on their significance.
5. When and where do you experience another culture's beauty? Reflect on the significance of these experiences to celebrating community.
6. Among your current or contemplated community involvements, where do you anticipate experiences of beloved community for your faith journey? Describe the character of the experiences you anticipate.

Epilogue

There never was a night or a problem that could defeat sunrise or hope.

—William Sloane Coffin, *Credo*

Hope is here, because God is here, and we are here! God outpours love and hope for us, for justice and beloved community now, and we respond now by . . .

What is our response? More personally, what is *your* response? The answer for all our tomorrows can be declared here and now. However, the answer will be *lived* day by day in all our tomorrows.

We come to this time with a vision that is God's dream of justice and beloved community. The vision is beautiful because hope and love are beautiful. The vision is inspiring because the deepest hunger of our hearts is for what we see. The vision is challenging because it calls for transformations that will disrupt in order to liberate and heal.

We come to this time with opportunities for our lives to answer yes to God's invitation to be a people for justice and beloved community. Whether in our neighborhoods or our nation or a distant land, God waits for us to answer and to live the vision. God's waiting merits our response. To ignore God's vision is to ignore God. What is your response?

We come to this time with spiritual practices to guide our commitment. In addition to the five spiritual practices highlighted as chapters in *Hope Is Here!* there are many other spiritual practices discussed within the chapters: singing, humility, suffering, growth, hospitality, study, invitation, forgiveness, friendship, sacrifice, Sabbath, pilgrimage, and protest. The practices are more than *information about* what is needed on the spiritual journey; the practices are *means of transformation* on and for the journey. Hope is in the practices, and the practices enliven us to experience people, situations, ourselves, and God with greater awareness of our purpose and the power of love.

The spiritual practices involve our bodies in the work for justice and beloved community. The practices mentor us as we traverse our souls' landscapes, and they lead us to realities that cause rejoicing, anger, fear, trauma, suffering, lament, courage, awe, wonder, laughter, devotion, understanding, and the full offering of ourselves. As never before, we will know what it means to love God with *all* our heart and with *all* our soul and with *all* our strength and with *all* our mind and our neighbor as ourselves (Luke 10:27, italics added). Spiritual practices help us to garner *all* of who we are to love.

Our faithful and tenacious enacting of the spiritual practices is essential for personal and social transformation. Prayer is not just to petition God to grant our desires. Prophetic remembering is more than uplifting speech about our inspiring faith tradition. Crossing boundaries of identity is not done only when positive outcomes are assured. Transforming conflict is not about overpowering adversaries. Celebrating community is not just to acknowledge successful achievements. If we ignore or distort how spiritual practices align with the necessities for justice and beloved community, then efforts for transformation will prove futile. A journey-bound people must *faithfully and persistently enact* the spiritual practices that empower them to pursue God's dream.

I hear people's anxiety and despair about the present and future state of the world. There are raging wars and threats for new outbreaks of war, environmental disasters, an ever-evolving pandemic, overt racism expressed in the media and public gatherings, unabated gun violence, rampant substance abuse, uncivil public discourse, a justice system biased against those who are poor, the assault on democratic institutions, the barrage of social media messages that promote lies and inflame hate, and the constant news that the world is falling apart. All this has led many to feel and say, "The times have never been this bad!"

Although I understand how people come to this conclusion, I also know that every generation has faced crises that threatened to rip apart their personal, social, and political foundations. Our ancestors have lived with slavery, plagues, poisoned air and rivers and dust-bowl land, economic depressions, discrimination, civil war, world wars, situations on the verge of nuclear war, political assassinations, vigilante hangings, White mob violence against envied Black communities, concentration camps, genocide, government and social indifferences to their plight, and a legion of uncertainties about a better future. We insult our ancestors by exclaiming we are overwhelmed and incapacitated because we live in the worst of times.

This is our season! This is our time! We cannot use the increased complexity of our times and lives as an excuse to withdraw from our distinctive challenges. Every generation has dealt with confusing new realities that led to bewildering circumstances.[1] Every generation has had the challenges and opportunities to embrace the work of hope. *This is our time! This is our season! Hope is here to enliven us to life and the practices for justice and beloved community.*

Beloved community experiences are described throughout *Hope Is Here!* These experiences are *signs* that point to God's vision of justice and beloved community. The signs depict and enliven us for the work of hope and love. *This is our season to create signs of justice and beloved community.* We, our churches, our neighborhoods, our communities, and our world need the signs. The signs point the way.

The needs for justice and beloved community are so numerous and complex that people who are impatient for change see current signs as insufficient evidence for hopefulness. Even when they see public protests or new legislation or more organizations devoted to their causes, their focus on the unaddressed remaining issues of their causes leaves them cynical about the significance of current signs of transformation. This attitude fails to understand that what is most despairing to those who suffer injustice and oppression is the absence of hopeful signs. The absence of signs elicits feelings of utter abandonment. I wrote in chapter 1, "The human spirit can endure the most horrific circumstances of life . . . except possibly the protracted feeling of utter abandonment." People who suffer oppression and injustice are often resigned to the reality that circumstances will not change immediately or perhaps even within their lifetimes. Still, they can experience hope when they see signs that compassion and justice will come. Generations have endured slavery, poverty, discrimination, fascism, and other suffocating realities because they saw signs of hope in abolitionists or in their children or in protests or in organizations that resisted the oppression. Signs of hope encourage people to live their times with hopefulness.

Each one of us can be a sign of hope for this and future seasons. Our efforts can inspire and encourage us as we seek to inspire and encourage others. We come to this time with the vision. We come to this time with opportunities and spiritual practices to enact the vision. We come to this time with God's desire that we be a sign for justice and beloved community.

Even with the promise that hope is here, the demands of the journey can intimidate us. We could give ourselves to scaling down the vision to something less challenging. But this is not how God dreams the vision. We recognize that the responsibilities for beloved community will consume our time and energy. Not only will our priorities and behaviors change, but we will change. The enormity of this sacred purpose can trigger our emotions. Uncertainty and anxiety evoke questions about the quest. Are we able and willing to give what is necessary to the transformative journey? Does God overestimate our capacities? Are there enough of us?

The questions and our anxiety would be especially understandable if the journey were taken without God and God's forces of hope and love. However, this is not our plight. God journeys with us! We should know what that means. If we do not know, be assured that the journey will answer our hearts.

The urgency for justice and beloved community is here and now! The efforts needed for transformation exceed the limits of my body. Still, I see the signs of hope all around me, and I am emboldened to persevere, even as I see the enormity of the challenges. In this time, on this journey, so many challenges and so many opportunities are mine . . . and yours. I anticipate continuing the journey with you. I know that our fellowship on the journey will make a difference for us and for our being a sign for so many others. I also know that however large our fellowship becomes, it alone will not be enough. What comforts and reassures me is knowing that the abiding presence and love of God on our journey is more than enough!

The spiritual wisdom of Victor Hugo speaks to my heart, and I believe every heart, to help us sustain our activism in all the coming days: "Courage, then, and patience! Courage for the great sorrows of life, and patience for the small ones. And then when you have laboriously accomplished your daily task, go to sleep in peace. God is awake."[2]

Notes

Chapter 1: Where Hope Abides

1. Reynolds Price, *A Whole New Life* (New York: Scribner Classics, 2000), 160.
2. Price, *A Whole New Life*, 184.
3. Price, *A Whole New Life*, 192.
4. Price, *A Whole New Life*, 186, 192.
5. Richard M. Cohen, *Strong at the Broken Places: Voices of Illness, a Chorus of Hope* (New York: HarperCollins, 2008), 1.
6. Howard Thurman, *The Mood of Christmas* (New York: Harper & Row, 1973; Richmond, IN: Friends United Press, 1985), 24.
7. Howard Thurman, *The Negro Spiritual Speaks of Life and Death* (New York: Harper & Row, 1947). Reprinted by Friends United Press in 1975 as a single volume with *Deep River*. The quote is from this single volume, 135. Italics have been added.
8. Pablo Neruda, *The Book of Questions*, trans. with introduction by William O'Daly (Port Townsend, WA: Copper Canyon Press, 2001), x.
9. Luther E. Smith Jr., "A Deep and Insatiable Hunger," in *Anchored in the Current: Discovering Howard Thurman as Educator, Activist, Guide, and Prophet*, ed. Gregory C. Ellison II (Louisville, KY: Westminster John Knox, 2020), 174.

Chapter 2: Hope's Work and Its Witnesses

1. Judith Herman, *Trauma and Recovery: The Aftermath of Violence—from Domestic Abuse to Political Terror* (New York: Basic Books, 1997), 153.
2. Nancy Eiesland, "Revealing Pain Undoes a Social Fiction," *Emory Report*, April 21, 2008, 7. Within a few months after the publication of this article, Nancy Eiesland was diagnosed with a terminal illness. Until the end of her life, she sought to stay available to the realities of family, friends, books, and the other passions of her life.

191

3. Howard Thurman, *Disciplines of the Spirit* (New York: Harper & Row, 1963; Richmond, IN: Friends United Press, 1977), 64–85.

Chapter 3: Contemplative Praying

1. Martin Luther King Jr., *Stride Toward Freedom: The Montgomery Story* (New York: Harper & Row, 1958), 134–35.
2. Bessel van der Kolk, *The Body Keeps the Score: Brain, Mind, and Body in the Healing of Trauma* (New York: Penguin Books, 2014), 285–86.
3. Brian Drayton and William P. Taber Jr., *A Language for the Inward Landscape: Spiritual Wisdom from the Quaker Movement* (Philadelphia: Tract Association of Friends, 2015), 68.
4. Parker Palmer, *Let Your Life Speak* (San Francisco: Jossey-Bass, 2000), 10.
5. Michael L. Birkel, *Silence and Witness: The Quaker Tradition* (Maryknoll, NY: Orbis Books, 2004), 63.
6. Abraham Joshua Heschel, as recounted by his daughter, Dr. Susannah Heschel, in *Following in My Father's Footsteps: Selma 40 Years Later*, published on "Safaria.org," www.sefaria.org/sheets/114324?lang=bi.
7. Joseph de Beaufort conversation with Brother Lawrence, https://img1.wsimg.com/blobby/go/1b49a5df-766c-4310-9f17-e0e412da5ae5/downloads/Faith-based%20Study%20of%20Brother_Lawrence.pdf?ver=1613886074486, 46-47.

Chapter 4: Prophetic Remembering

1. Adam Hochschild, *King Leopold's Ghost: A Story of Greed, Terror, and Heroism in Colonial Africa* (New York: Mariner Books, 1998), 294.
2. James W. Loewen, *Lies My Teacher Told Me: Everything Your American History Textbook Got Wrong*, 3rd ed. (New York: The New Press, 2018), 242.
3. Abraham Joshua Heschel, *Quest for God: Studies in Prayer and Symbolism* (New York: Crossroad Publishing, 1954), 138.
4. G. K. Chesterton, "Orthodoxy," in *The Chesterton Reader: 21 Works in One Volume* (Unexpurgated Edition) (Halcyon Press, 2009), Kindle edition, location 7314.
5. Luther E. Smith Jr., *Intimacy and Mission: Intentional Community as Crucible for Radical Discipleship* (Scottsdale, PA: Herald Press, 1994; Eugene, OR: Wipf and Stock, 2007), 156–57.

Chapter 5: Crossing Identity Boundaries

1. Dwayne Betts, *A Question of Freedom: A Memoir of Learning, Survival, and Coming of Age in Prison* (New York: Avery, 2009), 202, 203.
2. William F. May, *A Catalogue of Sins: A Contemporary Examination of Christian Conscience* (New York: Holt, Rinehart and Winston, 1967), 92.
3. Tim Kearney, "The Upside-Down Kingdom," in *The Prophetic Cry: Stories of Spirituality and Healing Inspired by L'Arche*, ed. Tim Kearney (Dublin: Veritas, 2000), 74.
4. Howard Thurman, *Disciplines of the Spirit* (New York: Harper & Row, 1963; Richmond, IN: Friends United Press, 1977), 127.

Chapter 6: Transforming Conflict

1. Jay Rothman, *Resolving Identity-Based Conflict: in Nations, Organizations, and Communities* (San Francisco: Jossey-Bass, 1997), 6, 7, 11.
2. Frederick Douglass, "West India Emancipation," August 3, 1857, in "(1857) Frederick Douglass, 'IF THERE IS NO STRUGGLE, THERE IS NO PROGRESS,'" BLACKPAST, January 25, 2007, https://www.blackpast.org/african-american-history/1857-frederick-douglass-if-there-no-struggle-there-no-progress/
3. RAND Corporation, https://www.rand.org/blog/rand-review/2016/01/course-correction-the-case-for-correctional-education.html.
4. Donald B. Kraybill, Steven M. Nolt, and David L. Weaver-Zercher, *Amish Grace: How Forgiveness Transcended Tragedy* (San Francisco: Jossey-Bass, 2007), 140.
5. Robert Ellsberg, "Père Jacques Bunol," in *All Saints: Daily Reflections on Saints, Prophets, and Witnesses for Our Time* (New York: Crossroad Publishing, 2004), 52.
6. Howard Thurman, *Disciplines of the Spirit* (New York: Harper & Row, 1963; Richmond, IN: Friends United Press, 1977), 120–21.

Chapter 7: Celebrating Community

1. John O'Donohue, *Beauty: The Invisible Embrace* (New York: Harper Perennial, 2004), 239.
2. Annie Dillard, *The Abundance: Narrative Essays Old and New* (New York: Harper-Collins, 2016), 181.
3. Evelyn Underhill, *Mysticism: A Study in the Nature and Development of Man's Spiritual Consciousness* (New York: Meridian, 1974), 258.
4. Fyodor Dostoevsky, *The Idiot*, trans. and ed. Alan Myers, introduction by William Leatherbarrow (New York: Oxford University Press, 1998), 400.
5. Rabbi Solomon of Karlin, quoted in Abraham Joshua Heschel, *The Sabbath: Its Meaning for Modern Man* (New York: Noonday Press, 1951), 74.

Epilogue

1. This criticism of interpreting current crises as "the worst of times" is also presented in my chapter, "Prophetic Vision and Its Radical Consequences." See *Reimagining Howard Thurman: The Unfinished Search for Common Ground*, ed., Walter Earl Fluker, (Maryknoll, NY: Orbis Books, 2023), 29.
2. Victor Hugo, *The Letters of Victor Hugo: From Exile, and after the Fall of the Empire*, ed. Paul Meurice (Boston and New York: Houghton Mifflin Co., 1898), 23.

Printed in the USA
CPSIA information can be obtained
at www.ICGtesting.com
JSHW011155010224
56484JS00001B/1